The Heart of All That Is:

Reflections on Home

Anthologies Published by Holy Cow! Press

The Heart of All That Is: Reflections on Home

Beloved on the Earth: 150 Poems of Grief and Gratitude

When Last on the Mountain: The View from Writers over 50

Ringing in the Wilderness: Selections from the North Country Anvil

The Frederick Manfred Reader

The Women's Great Lakes Reader

Strength to Your Sword Arm: Selected Writings by Brenda Ueland

Breaking Hard Ground: Stories of the Minnesota Farm Advocates

Walt Whitman: The Measure of His Song

Believing Everything: An Anthology of New Writing

Brother Songs: A Male Anthology of Poetry

The Heart of All That Is: Reflections on Home

Edited by Jim Perlman, Deborah Cooper, Mara Hart, Pamela Mittlefehldt

Holy Cow! Press :: Duluth, Minnesota :: 2013

Printed and bound in the United States of America.

Cover art by George Morrison, *Spirit Path, New Day, Red Rock Variation: Lake Superior Landscape*, 1990, acrylic and pastel on paper, 22 1/2 x 30 1/8 inches. Collection Minnesota Museum of American Art. Reprinted by permission of Briand Morrison, executor for the estate of George Morrison, and the Minnesota Museum of American Art.
Book design by Anton Khodakovsky.

ISBN 978-0-9859818-2-2

First printing, 2013
10 9 8 7 6 5 4 3 2 1

This project is supported in part by grant awards from the Ben and Jeanne Overman Charitable Trust, the Elmer L. and Eleanor J. Andersen Foundation, the Cy and Paula DeCosse Fund of the Minneapolis Foundation, The Lenfestey Family Foundation, and by generous gifts from individual donors.

Holy Cow! Press books are distributed to the trade by Consortium Book Sales & Distribution, c/o Perseus Distribution, 210 American Drive, Jackson, TN 38301.

For inquiries, write to:

Holy Cow! Press, Post Office Box 3170,
Mount Royal Station,
Duluth, MN 55803.

Please visit our website:
www.holycowpress.org

Table of Contents

The Heart of All That Is: Reflections on Home

Introduction

HOME. IS IT A PLACE OR A FACE? An address or a state of mind? Shelter or prison? Hearth or horizon? What does *home* mean in this twenty-first century?

Home is not static. It is a verb, as well as a noun, a description as well as a destination. Home is a dialectic, an oxymoron. Implicit in the grounding promised by the idea of home is the syncopated counterpoint of yearning—a longing to flee as well as an ache to return.

Home is not uncontested territory. To reflect on home challenges us to also confront homelessness. To claim home forces us to also acknowledge displacement and loss. To embrace home challenges us to also consider the imperative of flight.

Home is a topic that has been written about so extensively that it has generated its own lexicon of clichés, an entire alphabet of images and assumptions. There is little new that can be said about home—and perhaps that is the point. That home—however it is defined, wherever it is located—is "the heart of all that is." In spite of the complexity, the contradictions, the spectrum of emotional responses evoked by *home*, "home for most of us is the place we spend all our lives re-imagining," as Mark Vinz states in his essay, "Where in the World Did You Come from?"

It is those re-imaginings, the multi-layered, multi-faceted reflections on home, that we, the four editors of this book, wanted to hear. We had previously co-edited *Beloved: 150 Poems of Grief and Gratitude*, and were eager to collaborate on a new project, one focused this time on *home*. We put out an open-ended call for poems and essays on the idea of home—where it is located in one's life, how it may have changed over time, what it means. The response was a motherlode of images, definitions, descriptions, memories, interpretations, dreams. As we went through the process of sifting, sorting, selecting, we were repeatedly struck by the juxtaposition of common ground and unexpected territory, by the familiarity of images and the spark of a shining phrase.

The shape of the anthology emerged from the poems and essays themselves. As with most good stories, we begin at the beginning, in the AMBER WILDS OF CHILDHOOD, to lift a phrase from Catherine Hodges's poem "Safe." The kitchens, the cornfields, the rooftops, the secrets and the secret places, the "scratch and wrap" of family, to use Elizabeth Weir's wonderful phrase. This first section ends with Cary Waterman's words: "And finally, all that horizon which did not seem a limiting thing, the curve of a bowl, the furthest circumference. It seemed instead possibility, freedom, escape."

And as we respond to the call of the horizon, we find ourselves far and way from home, clutching FOLDED MAPS OF THE PAST. Home is seen in a rearview mirror or from "a distant ship tiding home," as Bruce Pratt writes. Here the question "where are you from?" evokes a chorus of memories and places: Lodz, Nowy Sacz, Piraeus, Owatonna. "I am Africa misplaced," Emily Bright exclaims. There is warning here. "A body shouldn't go too far from home," says Bosaina, the Egyptian *ama* of Tami Mohamed Brown's "Portrait Without Words." And there is a call for blessing: "Help me to remember/all of our lost lands, help me to sing," Joseph Bruchac sings for us all in "Lands of Song."

Perhaps we only truly know home by LIVING A SECOND TIME IN MEMORY, as Sarah Weitzman suggests, looking back at home from the perspective of time, distance and age. The work in this section in part responds to Claudia Reder's question, "what is the meaning of things?" The poems and essays here honor the *stuff* of home: old photos and report cards, wedding albums, a portable Singer, potato salad, battered volumes of Dickens—the things that hold us together, that Laura Hansen compares to the dust adhering like fingerprints that identify us.

Here home often only remains in memory, part of our bulldozed past that still continues to shape us. Connie Wanek reflects on this interplay of past and present, place and self, in her poem, "Pecans": "A place is both itself/and what we make of it, as we are ourselves and what a place makes of us." This section ends with Judith Prest's haunting question: "who will know this land/when we are gone?"

But home is not always a place of treasured memories or sustaining myth, as the poems and essays in Seeking Shelter remind us. For myriad reasons, many are without a place to call home. This section opens with Ethna McKiernan's haunting jeremiad, "Dear God of H_____," addressing the "desolate/blessed God of homelessness." Included here are portraits of individuals, like Fran Markover's "Chicken Charlie" and the children in Julie Landsman's fourth grade classroom. These pieces challenge us to face the reality Freya Manfred describes when she writes that if you have no home, you are left "with the horror of the world around you." Jessica Erica Hahn offers a different perspective on the notion of home in her essay, "Passing Through: Squatting is Another Name for Home." Home in this section is not always a place of welcome or possibility. Roberta J. Hill writes of being on a threshold, where her brown face dictates a lack of welcome in a neighborhood, while M.J. Fievre describes her attempt to find her home in post-earthquake Haiti. And yet, as Deborah Cooper drives home from her poetry class at the jail, the moon that her students wrote about before returning to their blocks for lockdown "sails the darkening canopy of sky/from wide horizon/to horizon."

If home is in part a search for the past, an act of memory, it is also an act of faith, an affirmation, a claiming. Where the Rain Returns celebrates those places that have become our metaphors, as Mary Kay Rummel writes in "Between," the places where the rain returns, where we are claimed by place. The poems and essays here are celebrations of place and belonging. This section is rich with the specific images that have claimed us: Sitka spruce forests, Rummel's' "fields of shuck and stack," Amy Nash's New England dirt, /the taste of beets out back," Sherry Rovig's "granite boulders/and black raspberries." These are pieces about arrival, about settling, about being lured home—about finding "a nest in the branches of your arms," Gary Boelhower writes to his beloved. "My country is this dirt/that gathers under my fingernails…" Ellie Schoenfeld proclaims. Home ground.

The final section, THE CONTOURS OF PRIVATE GEOGRAPHY, draws its name from Cynthia Baer's "Fault Lines." The writings here muse on the meaning of home. Some pieces address the complexity of the question, what does it mean to be native to this place, a question raised eloquently in Keiko Lane's "Along Highway 1." Is home "a complete sentence," as Miriam Weinstein states? Or is it a question mark? Is home more about memory and yearning, or about being firmly grounded? J P. White offers some resolution to these questions, suggesting that home is a place where we are all "A little bit lost. A little bit found."

Home is "a messy topography, " Ellen Shriner observes. It is both "challenge and cradle," as Heather McGrew notes. Our beliefs about home are a promise— and a lie: "Home meant magic, where children could be held/safe," Joyce Lombard writes in "Rituals of December," even as bombs are falling from the sky.

We are all somehow "tattoed by place," Amy Jo Swing proclaims, "every inch etched in the skin". This collection is about such places: specific places—Alaska, the Black Hills, the hills of Pennsylvania. It is also about lost places: migration, destruction, ruin. What does it mean to be native to some place? What does it mean to be home?

As we reflected on the wealth and range of responses to our initial questions, and crafted the order and shape of the book, we were also seeking its title. What is this book truly about? The answer came clear as we considered a reference to the Lakota name for the Black Hills that Kristina Roth made in her essay "Directions Home." *Se Hapa*: *The Heart of All That Is.* However it is defined, wherever it is located, however it has formed or failed us, home is at the heart of our being.

Collected here is a kaleidoscopic refraction of *home*: a photograph, a song, a clock marking time. An unfinished map. A ruin. An empty lot. Fear in a basement or the promise of the view from a rooftop.

In Arabic, the word *bayt* refers to both a house and a line of poetry. And so perhaps home is best described as a dwelling "made of curved words," as Farzana Marie describes it in "Where We Dwell." We invite you to enter these houses made of words. Welcome home.

Pamela Mittlefehldt
June, 2013

I

The Amber Wilds of Childhood:

In the Beginning

The House Made of Words

James Cihlar

If I could take the moment by the throat,
I would pin it down to paper.
Someone's got to do it,
set the words in order.

When I was six, my home was not
the long living room
filled with cigarette smoke,
the blue eye at the end.

It was there on the front seat
between me and my father
as we took a drive at night
around the bluffs outside the city,
the green glow of the dashboard
reflecting on our faces.

We carried *home* with us,
into the booth at the truck stop,
Loretta Lynn and Hank Williams
on the wall-jukebox at our table.

When my father left for good
the words spilled like ink
off the edges of the paper.
It would be years before
I began to pick them up
and lay them in a line.

Someone's got to do it,
shake the moment
by the collar
and say, Learn.

Some day I will have
a house made of words.
It will be all windows and doors,
with the words placed in rows,
each one leading to the next,
the way the present
wears the face of the past.

The home stretch

Karen Lynn Erickson

I think twice now about tight places
steering wheels loom large
school desks and restroom stalls present new corners
my clothes shrink from week to week
breathing bumps against a hard round dome
and my socks are far, far away

My office now is cut in half
Next to my desk a cradle waits
Scarred bookshelves peer at new white furniture
computer disks nestle in stacks of tiny shirts
I make room week by week

Last night I dreamed of running
light on my feet on an open road
I woke to feel a kick and my whole belly moved
Did you dream, too, and run in your warm bed?
Tight within and tight without
we squeeze and swell toward
contraction and mysterious flights

When you knock in the tightest place
of all I'll dream of a wide expanse
and a house with many rooms

A Home Worth Remembering

Kathleen Weihe

You gave me the world and since then, it being so large a gift, almost a a burden, I've tried to box it up, bring it into size. The rules were simple at first. Wander no further, I told myself, than the stone wall at the edge of the cemetery. Dig no deeper than what you can stand in and still see out of. Climb no higher than the limb that curves in on itself. This outer world was mine—the space between the garage and the lilacs; the cement cornerstones; the green, tidy, complete world offered up by the front porch light at night. Each day I pushed further into the yards and public lands around me, an advent calendar opening door by door, tree by tree.

The smooth-skinned salamander with the blunt, beautiful fingers of a rubber baby I enclosed in the soft box of my palms and took to an old stone grill. I built it a home worth remembering and kept it until one day it must have gone hand over hand up the chimney and away. A black cat came in the winter. I built it a house of plywood against the fence and in the snowy afternoons that sifted without warning into night we hunched over a fire in the small house, burning the leaves that hung on past fall. I watched the snow float past the slant of wooden roof, watched one long weed after another bending in or away, in and away, brushing the wind's rhythm against the edge of home.

Corn Rows

Morgan Grayce Willow

One by one,
before they were even three,
he'd set them down
and say, "If you get lost,
just follow the corn row,
the one you're in.
Don't cross over.
The row you're in.
Take it all the way
out to the fence."

Out front in the yard
he'd point to the grove.
"That's north," he'd say.
"The barn here, that's east.
The barn is always east of the house.
The creek's behind us,
so that means south.
That don't change.
Same with the corn:
north-south; east-west."

At night, he'd work them
on the North Star and the Big Dipper;
daytime the sun's path.
"The shadow of the corn
never points south. Can't.
The sun is at its back."

Corn was check planted
in those days, wires
guiding the planter.
From any place you'd stand,
straight lines up the hills,
straight lines down. Nowadays,
no fence rows. No lines.
No more north.

"Find your way to the barn,"
he used to say. "Then you'll know
exactly where you're at."

Thoughts Upon Returning Home to an English Spring

After Jim Moore

Elizabeth Weir

Mists of cow parsley massed under chestnuts
smell as immediate as childhood—
no one knows how to love the way I do
the scent of syringa outside my girlhood window,
the wag in our dog's bottom when we pedal home
from school, our mother's voice irritable from
the constant scrimp and save of life, our kitchen
warm with the promise of baked jam tarts;
the black-silk-feel of Trevor's tea-drinking rabbit,
as he laps from my brother's china saucer;
little Nicky, clamoring to tell an endless story,
us arguing, loud and daft, over who reads
the Beano comic first; Mummy relaxing in the curl
of her after-tea cigarette and our quiet dad
wreathed in clouds of worry about money; me,
climbing the stairs and loving the feeling of falling
asleep in the scratch and wrap of family, Danny,
the cat, snugged tight in the crook of my knees.

The Stradivarius in the Locker

Keith Gunderson

Any family that had an apartment at 3142 Lyndale Ave. So. also had a locker in the basement where they could store all the junk they couldn't use and wouldn't throw away and in the big pile of junk in our locker I found a little brown violin with no strings and one crack and which looked sort of pretty when you wiped the dust off so I asked my Dad about it because he was a terrific piano player and almost became a piano teacher and knew everything about music and had studied music at The McPhail School of Music and he told me I should be careful when I fooled around with the violin because it might be a Strad ... and then I couldn't understand what he'd said so I asked him what he'd said it might be so he said the same word again so I had to ask him again and then he said very slowly it might be a STRAD I VAR I US which he said was a violin made by the best violin maker in the history of the world and if we had one it would be worth a fortune and one of these days he'd take it down to Schmitt's Music store to see if it was a STRADIVARIUS which it probably was and he'd cash it in and we'd move out of this dump but my Mom said that if that violin was a Stradivarius our TV set was a CHIPPENDALE and I didn't ask her what she meant but my Dad asked her what SHE knew about it and she said she didn't know anything about violins but she knew a lot about Dad so then I knew what she'd meant and we both laughed and even Dad laughed too because he couldn't help it though at the end of his laugh he snuck in a little heh heh heh he could help and said that after he cashed the violin in he'd send her a postcard from the Bahama Islands where he'd be retiring and my Mom said I'll be waiting Dad I'll be waiting and don't forget to send last month's rent with the postcard and when he finally got around to checking out the violin it wasn't a Stradivarius or even a Chippendale but we'd moved out of the dump anyway but I'd loved 3142 Lyndale Ave So. for such a long time I didn't know why my Dad had called it a dump anymore than I first knew what he meant when he called the violin a Stradivarius.

Keep Out

Julia Morris Paul

You fixate on the brick arch
above the door.
What was it your parents
told you about its keystone?
A story to convince you
of its magic. *Make a wish,*
when you cross the threshold,
it will be granted.
And you believed that
for almost forever,
like a lot of things
before the shouting matches
curled the wallpaper
and the mildew
of silence sprouted.
You were still a girl
when sheets were thrown
over the furniture
and gravel pinged a farewell
song against the underside
of the Fairlane.
Now wildflowers tiptoe
toward the massive oak door.
The steps are gone.
The posted sign warns:
Danger. Keep Out.
Black-eyed Susans
and Queen Anne's lace
hover, coy, tilting heads,
like beauty flirting with danger,
like you.

Drawing of My Family: Age Six

Jill Breckenridge

One cloud above a white house,
one mother, a little girl,
a father sitting in his blue car
as the cloud rains under itself.

In my childhood drawing, a sidewalk
reaches from the front door to a road
where the car drives away.

Black smoke curls out of the chimney,
black V birds flap away from the tree,

the blue sky doesn't leave, nor the mother
in her red coat with twelve buttons,
all of them fastened, even the one

under her round head, turned away
from the father and daughter.

The windows wear capital-R-shaped curtains,
and the doorknob is colored black,
drawn big enough that a good father,
if he forgot his key, could open
the front door and come home,

but if it's night and he's the bad father,
he won't be able to see the doorknob
until tomorrow when the good father returns.

A gray cat should be colored in, hunting
mice to hide under the kitchen table,
and a red cocker spaniel, old and fussy,
biting company because his ears hurt.

The little girl should be running
across the yard yelling, "Hurry up!"
to her baby brother, not in the picture
because he isn't born for three more years,
but she misses him already.

It should be raining all over this picture,
not just under the single white cloud,
raining on the mother in her red coat
until she looks toward the little girl,

raining on the father's car until
he stops driving and walks back
to stand on the green strip of yard

with the mother and daughter,
so they'll all be smiling big smiles,
way up above their ears,
like they already are in this picture.

Child with Reader

Elisabeth Murawski

The little girl's learning to read.
The book's about a family
on Pleasant Street, their house

not at all like the basement flat
she lives in, a furnace hulking mid-
kitchen, no tub. In winter

the landlord will interrupt a meal
to shovel coal. He's Russian, proud
of the scar on his forehead

from the revolution. His white
hair, short and stubbly, reminds her
of the dog she teased, poked at

through a gate she thought locked.
His fur stood on end.
He broke free and chased her.

The girl shuts the book, still
troubled by the silent w
in "answer." On Pleasant Street

no one dreams as she did
of a skeleton in top hat and tuxedo.
No one trembles at the light-

fingered dark. She runs to her tree.
The landlord's smoking on his porch.
She knows he is watching.

In the Basement

Molly Sutton Kiefer

Running a bath, the father reels against
his daughter. She refuses to enter the water,
wriggles, a slippery peach.

His day has been longer and his glasses
slip in the water, fish-plunk. This is opportunity
to scuttle. Her braids are long ropes, leaving a trail.

She is flying now, punished into
the basement, bare bottom on wooden step.
Who knows what is beneath her?

The door makes a locking sound, a click
that causes her groan and somewhere, there is rustling.
A black cat or the slime of a slug beneath her.

How weightless her body becomes, how
quiet the air. She has become forgotten.
She will not move, not ever.

Slow to take shape: old Christmas tree, smell
of pine, slit eye of furnace. When she is older, she will
remember, will have to go into the basement:

ornaments, filter. She will look at the ceiling in wide
memory, find the smell of soap on her hands,
think of drowning in the dark.

Prairie World and Wanderer

Margaret Hasse

Big bluestem and sedge, goldenrod and sunflower
gave us as children a place to go from light to dim,
from dun to emerald, exposed to hidden.
Above us, grasses displayed seeds to the sun.

When we were quiet, the small breeze and insects
made sounds as if saying *wish on this,*
A bird cried *come to me, come to me.*
The fields made a many-chambered house.

Pressing plants down, we carpeted floors.
In one room, we ate our sandwiches.
At the end of a tunneled corridor
we took naps, once finding where a deer

had tamped a sleeping space, still warm.
Once, we came across a stand of milkweed
with knots of sap in their umbels.
Ornaments hung from branches,

something folded inside, a drop that trembled
like a silent bell and broke, releasing
a butterfly with darning thread for feet.
The stained glass windows of its wings opened.

It was a monarch who dried its wings
of white, black, and orange until
it could flutter like a tiny flag into the blue
beyond our mansion with its roof of air.

Prairie Sundown, North Dakota

John Sorensen

I give you the shadow of a farmhouse,
lying quietly on the evening prairie.
The shadow reaches across the long grass of the farmyard,
edging toward the road,
ignoring the barbed wire fence that holds back the ditch.
The shadow moves, the southeast sky darkens, and the sun drops lower
behind the house, behind Uncle Carl's granary,
sinking toward the fields beyond.

With supper over, cousins run together again.
We were cowboys by day in the coulee and the pasture;
now we hunt frogs in the cooling grass.
When nearly the entire yard is in the shadow of the house,
I walk to the middle of the road, to the softened roofline of the house.
I plant my feet on the shadow ridge of the house
and call to my sisters, my brother, my cousins,
Look! I'm standing on top of the house!
I admire my own shadow, stretching
down the ditch and up, falling across the
wheat stalks of the next field.
I have never felt so tall.

I turn back for full appreciation of how high up
I am, judging the distance to the house. City kid, I call to
the fathers sitting, smoking on the south porch
in the fading sun. Look! I call, I'm standing on top of the house!
They cannot hear me or understand me, but my uncle waves.
Uncle Marvin. I watched him working in the shop

today. Hammering orange metal, fixing the tractor.
You're not on the house, you're in the air! a cousin
shouts. You're falling to the ground!
I look down. My feet rest in sunlit gravel.
The roof has moved out from under me. I jump
with both feet toward the ridge, amazed the shadow has moved so fast,
glad I've safely reached it again. The others join me,
and we are a row of five tall, thin, figures
on the ridgeline of the house.
One of us extends a hand toward the lightning rod at the peak.
Another shouts, Don't touch that! You'll get killed!
Too late, he touches the rod, quivers with electricity,
then dies, falls off the peak of the house, rolls across the road,
into the ditch.
We all laugh and follow,
walking the ridgeline to the lightning rod, touching,
quivering, dying,
rolling dead
into the dusty grass of the ditch.

A father shouts. We'd had baths.

We'd had baths, in galvanized tubs behind the house,
and the prairie dust of that day's play
had been washed away and
returned to the ground,
just as the house itself has been returned,
ashes and hardware and the yard itself, now covered over
by a field of wheat.

The house's shadow, of course, remains.
It appears each cloudless summer evening,
just as the shadow of this poem is yours
though this paper be turned to dust.

Walk with me.
Step carefully now, lest you slip and fall.
Balance; hold out your arms as you walk
the ridgeline. And please, promise me that when you
reach the peak and you touch
the lightning rod,
you will die.
And we, each of us, will touch, die, and follow,
never mind the grownups' concern for baths,
as we fall into shadows
of houses and granaries and aunts and uncles
now gone.

Hometown

Robin Chapman

Which way was north?
Oak Ridge's directions were valley-skewed,
the long run of the road a compass needle.
The hills insistent
on the ways of water,
every fold a creek.

Which way was right?
The right was science-skewed,
the long miles of buildings
devoted to their task of sorting molecules,
pulling the small handfuls of death
out of the tons of yellowcake.

Which way was left?
What's left was mercury running into the creek,
the long mile of river, the roots of the trees.
What's begun always has its own logic,
runs like a clock, like stockpiles,
keeping them up.

Which way was true?
The long run of childhood was twilight
and heat, summer shimmering in the concrete pool.
The game had rules—not to be found,
and the black widow spider
another neighbor we knew to give space to.

Which way was danger?
The spider's eye refracted the high tension towers
that carried the power of the Tennessee River in flood
to the task of making nuclear weapons.
Here the intent to save
the world.

Which way was love?
At the Overlook, in old cars,
we kissed and kissed, the body's pull
an insistence—sap and root,
another place to view
the only home we knew.

Safe

Catherine Abbey Hodges

I am six. I don't like coffee,
but the smell of it drifting
up the stairs
along with breakfast-making clatter
        means I'm safe.
                I lie in bed, point
my toes, think about the secret
language I'm making, my list
of words and their meanings.
Today I'll write them in the book
I plan to make with sheets
of my mother's onion skin
        typing paper.
                The summer I turn
nine, my father will find
a bat, rust-colored and furred,
roosting among the loquats
in our back yard. The breathing
fact of a wild creature so near
        will alarm and thrill me.
                By then, my private
language will be long forgotten,
not to be remembered until
I'm forty and look back to glimpse
myself safe in the amber
        wilds of my childhood,
first and last speaker
        of a snatch of language
                without a name.

Shelling Peas

FOR MY MOTHER

Penny Harter

We're shelling peas, gently rocking on the swing
that hangs on chains from the roof of the porch
at my grandparents' house.

I'm four years old, wedged between Mother and Nana.
Singing as we swing, I balance a metal pot on my knees
as peas rattle into it from their nimble hands.

Newly picked from the garden out back, the pods are still
warm from the sun. I take pleasure in the sudden give
along each seam, the stream of peas into my waiting palm.

Now and then I eat a handful, sweet-bitter on my tongue,
savoring their rawness, the scent of earth, the mystery
of taste revealed as I crunch their hard round bodies.

Feet not touching the floor, eyes even with the lattice-work
under the porch railing, I sway and dream in the shifting
light and shade of a long summer afternoon.

The owl and the pussycat went to sea / in a beautiful pea-green boat,
my mother recites to me at bedtime, her weight on the side of my bed,
her voice almost chanting this poem she has loved since childhood.

A blessing in my mouth, those pale, hard peas, which I taste
even now as I chew on this memory, hungry for a pea-green boat
I might go out to sea in, trawling for light among the watery stars.

Horizon

Cary Waterman

"Pursuing the horizon without interruption inevitably prohibits landfall, harbor, home..."

—Angus Fletcher
A New Theory for American Poetry

I go to the apartment roof alone and always look west, inland toward the lime-green hills of the Connecticut valley in spring and summer and the burnt colors of fall. I could have looked east—over the tenements and factories of Bridgeport to Long Island Sound and Seaside Park with its bathhouse and rocky beaches. I could have looked to the sunrise, but didn't. I looked west, the horizon unreachable, enclosing and not enclosing. What was beyond those hills? And what was I really seeking, up on the roof of the four-story apartment building alone, walking boards laid down over black tar?

* * *

I am a fat, fingernail-biting girl—the bloody nails, flabby arms, thick unruly hair that will not lie flat. I go to the edge, look down, imagine falling, then flying. It is not impossible. I would jump. And I would fly. Or, at least summersault and land on my feet. There are pigeons roosting. Slate-grey birds with feathers the color of oil slick. One day in third grade, the boy behind me taps my back and when I turn he holds out the severed pigeon head he has made into a finger puppet on his dirty hand.

I wear the apartment key on a string around my neck. Once I lost the key and my mother was sure someone would find their way to our apartment door even though there were hundreds of doors, each one identical to the next. After that, I would go to another apartment after school one floor up where 'Aunt' Maude lived and wait for my mother. Aunt Maude had a life-sized statue of the Virgin Mary in her bedroom. The Virgin, hands outspread, stood on the earth, her feet crushing the snake. I wanted a statue like that. Aunt Maude also had a bright red kitchen and Victorian loveseats and chairs. It was all so neat. Once I arrived at her door, legs crossed and having to pee. I ran to the bathroom, leaving a trail of mud I would have to get on hands and knees to clean up.

* * *

I was not afraid on the roof and I didn't jump. I was surrounded by other brick apartment buildings, each one a colossus along Washington Avenue. The Sanford, where one-eyed Peter's father was the Super. And the Fleetwood, where Joe Black's mother worked. He was older than most of us kids and had dark eyes and black hair. One day he offered to ride me on his bike all the way to Seaside Park but I was afraid of him and ran away. He was taken away one night after he chased his mother up and down the halls with a butcher knife and was sent to Newtown, the hospital for the insane where my mother threatened she would end up if I didn't behave.

My mother told people we were Cliff Dwellers, hoping to evoke images of Manhattan's Riverside Drive, not the ruins of the Anasazi. She said this to give an air of luxury to the fact that four people (mother, father, brother, and me), one collie, one parakeet, and, for a few months, two rabbits that ate the kitchen linoleum were crammed into a one-bedroom apartment. This was the same apartment my parents had moved to as newlyweds, and the apartment in which my brother and I (and our stillborn sister) were conceived, and the apartment our father returned to after his Marine glory days stationed in Honolulu during WWII, eligible for the GI Bill providing low-cost home mortgages with no down payment. But we did not buy a house. We looked at houses. We spent decades of afternoons and weekends driving around with realtors. But my mother would not choose. Something was always wrong. A hill in the backyard where there could be mud slides. Not enough windows. Too many windows. Way out in the suburbs. Too close to the city. Not a colonial. Not this…not that. No, no, no, no. I begged and pleaded. I cried for my own room. No. No. No. Finally I gave up. The apartment became my mother's (and my) particular hell where I would live until I was eighteen and left for college. That was also the year my parents would finally buy a house.

* * *

Our building was U-shaped, two gargoyle wings jutting from the entryway. It had once been fancy with brass railings and a lighted foyer with a bank of mailboxes, each with its own little key. But the building was beginning to run down. The white subway tiled floors weren't washed as often. The super spent most days in the basement by the coal furnace with his cronies sitting around and drinking beer. He had cordoned off a little clubroom with a card table and chairs and hung girlie calendars on the walls. Everything was dirty and when I went to the basement to get my bike, if he was there I'd look away as I passed the pinups. If he wasn't, I'd stop and stare, titillated by the fleshy women, breasts and buttocks spilling out into coal dust.

In our apartment, the first room off the hall was the bedroom where my brother and I slept opposite each other in twin beds we had to sidle around. My mother slept on the couch and my father on a rollaway in the living room. For a long time there was a crib in the bedroom with a mesh top that could be latched to keep a child in. It was used for clothes storage. There was also a baby carriage jammed up against my bed. It too was filled with outgrown stuff. Every spring my mother would drive a load to the Little Sisters of the Poor but the piles continued to grow and consume the room. The closet was packed and had over-the-door hangers on both sides for more clothes to hang.

The bathroom was the only room with a lock. I spent a lot of time in there, protected by the lock on one side and the bubbled window on the other. I would stand on the edge of the bathtub and look at my breasts in the mirror over the sink. Compare myself to the pin-ups Mr. Haskell had in the basement.

The living room had a couch, two tiered maple end tables, assorted chairs, a dining room table, the old black telephone, a high chair and playpen when my brother was little, a black and white TV, and the folded up bed my father slept on. My mother would paint this room several times when my father was gone for the weekend skiing, always making it darker and darker from tan to Hunter green to finally, maroon.

At Christmas my father and brother would lay down a big piece of plywood in the middle of the living room for my brother's American Flyer train. He had boxcars and coal cars and a log dump car and a red caboose and a station that lit up and an engine with a horn and headlight that could blow smoke. I can't remember how we navigated the living room at Christmas, the four of us and the dog, the decorated tree, the train going around and around.

* * *

Perhaps my mother, a petite redhead, enjoyed the attention of the realtors. This idea that only occurs to me now makes my mother's inability to buy a house more acceptable. These men were obsequious, if frustrated with her. She was lonely, and, as she often told me, felt unappreciated. There was power in being the potential buyer, even though she never bought. Her favorite was Mr. Ryan. She drove around with him looking at houses for twenty years. I remember one of the hundreds we looked at. It was a brand new split-level and had wall-to-wall carpet, a mudroom, and a balcony in the living room where you could look down when you came out of your bedroom. But there was a hill in the backyard, not too close to the house. What was over that hill? My father, who rarely came with us, liked this house and he and my mother fought about it. She said who would want to come into a house through a mudroom. And what about mudslides from that hill? For some reason I have forgotten, I took my mother's side in the argument and can still see the disgusted I-give-up look on my father's face. I remember it because I knew at the time I was wrong, that the argument was not about the house. It was about power and I was playing sides and the side I wanted to be on was my mother's. But why? Or was I just arguing for the sake of argument? Arguing to see if I could win. My father used to say I would make a good lawyer. But really, it was all about losing.

* * *

The U-shaped apartment roof was covered with boardwalk that led to laundry lines. Cold December afternoons, my mother, her hands angry-red, would ride the elevator carrying her wicker basket of wet laundry, then climb the last flight of stairs to the roof to hang our clothes, sheets and towels. She would curse coming back later to find the laundry covered with black dots of soot from the big chimneys that heated the building and made the radiators clang. She cursed about a lot of things—my father's drinking, my ungratefulness, my loud voice, my taking up too much space. *Judas Priest* was her favored expression and one that, attending Catholic school, confused me. When she was really angry she'd threaten to leave and take my brother but leave me with my father. We were alike, she said. We deserved each other.

* * *

I never had friends come home with me. Through high school, I met my dates outside on the street and kissed them goodbye in their cars. I never invited anyone to the roof. There was a shelter up there with a bench facing predictably east, sunrise, new day. I sat there one night with my father after another violent argument with my mother, perhaps the one when I kicked out the glass of a mirror that was propped up against the cramped bedroom wall. I fled the stifling apartment, ran down the dirty hallway to the elevator, pushed the button and rose up before climbing the last flight of stairs to the roof. My father came up later and sat with me. He said my mother was changing. I don't know if he actually called it the *change of life*. I wouldn't have known what that was. But I was changing, too. My mother would dry up as I was beginning to bleed every month into possibility, my poor father in-between us, a fulcrum of sorts, except that he would become more and more absent to Ski Club meetings or bowling at the Algonquin Club before adjourning to the bar.

I could not be patient. I loved my mother. And, I hated her. I was surrounded and adrift. After my father and I looked out to the sea and he tried to reason with me, he left and I turned to look west. What was out there, all those miles and miles of fields and hills, all that landscape? And finally, all that horizon which did not seem a limiting thing, the curve of a bowl, the furthest circumference. It seemed instead possibility, freedom, escape.

II

Folded Maps of the Past:
Far and Away from Home

Going Home

Rosemary Winslow

There is no going home
as usual
the vehicle stalls
in reverse gear
in mud tracks

as essential as
the flat fields, the blades
of shadowed pines over the drive,
the sun bleeding
from the west.

On the rise the house,
painted clapboard, the color of cream,
is rented now like bodies
of water and minerals made
living by some miracle

which is to say some process
we don't understand.
Some day we'll have a
different owner,
a different lover,

pines trees and whirling wind,
that primitive communion,
a new testament
of each generation.

All going home is never going back—
there may be ruin and mud tracks
deep to make wheels spin. The only way
is slogging on,
or else walking
on water.

Or yet it may be dry,
the sand flying in your nostrils
but you must breathe, must go, must go
on, which is to say, go on making
required visits, like stations

of a cross. It is a way
of finding what we lost
or never had, of learning we are only
renters, and making new covenants,
going where we belong.

Leaving

Emily Ruth Hazel

Before the roosters rouse, we're on the road,
our headlights pointing homeward.
Silos and barns appear and disappear,
dissolving in the fog
as our lone, white Caravan climbs
the rolling hills you know so well,
your large hands easy on the wheel, guiding us
through the skim milk mist of morning.
Over the cornfields, the cream-colored sun
slides across the skillet of the sky
like butter warming, its edges yellowing
as it melts. The day stretches
long before us, between the night
we're half-pretending hasn't passed,
our pillows pressed against the window glass,
and the night we're moving toward—
one that is waiting to blanket us
as soon as we arrive. On the other side of day,
there won't be any fireflies
sparking in the glistening grass,
but a teal blue door will open for us
with a twist of the key
that dangles just above your knee and gently
sways to the rise-and-fall rhythm of these
Ohio roads. The map of your past
now quietly folded away, home lies before you
and yet remains behind. From time to time,
you glance at the rear view mirror

as if to remember the route,
its swells and dips and curves—
your brown eyes always returning
to the road ahead, taking it all in.
You look beyond the painted lines
at what I've come to call my own
because it first belonged to you—
here, this generous spread,
familiar earth and undivided sky.

Relearning Home

Heather McGrew

I remember a time when my only home was Minnesota, when the map of my world was so small that if I had sketched it out, it would have fit into my back pocket without being folded even once. Our house on Elm Street in Owatonna was the center of my world, and for me that world extended no further than five miles in any direction. Just down the street from the house a creek ran across the land, and I spent many hours there with my sister Dawn digging for crawfish. We'd often bring a few home and keep them in a cage for a while, but once one pinched my finger tightly so I threw it across the yard and never saw it again.

Across from the house was a large field I was certain had been cleared for the sole purpose of creating a space for kids to run and play. On the other side of that lay a cemetery through which Dawn and I would ride our bikes almost daily to get to the Kwik Trip, where we'd buy penny candy, ride further on to the tennis courts with the candy stuffed in our cheeks, and watch people play until the sun started to drop. Then we'd turn our bikes around, point them back in the direction of home, and ride back to that place where everything began and ended.

That was life as a third grader, filled with crawfish and penny candy and fast bike rides through the cemetery before it got too dark. My world was simple and small enough: I knew all the streets, landmarks, neighbors. My bike could take me anywhere I needed to go, and Dawn beside me on her bike was enough for companionship, and a dollar or two in my pocket was enough for entertainment, and if anyone asked me where home was I could answer in three seconds flat.

We left Elm Street when I finished third grade but stayed within the boundaries of Minnesota until I graduated from high school. It was 1993 when an airplane took me to England, the place where I first realized my idea of home had become undeniable muddled. Four months—a full college semester—had been set aside for reading Thomas Hardy and Charles Dickens with English grass beneath my back. I left Minnesota with a group of twenty other students, a professor, and his family; collectively, we formed a group called The England Termers. A 15th century building called Hengrave Hall was to serve as our point of orientation, the only place that we'd return to on a regular basis during our travels.

I remember first entering the grounds of Hengrave. Our Welsh bus driver, Alec, maneuvered us carefully through the gate that introduced it. I quickly spotted two things after we'd cleared the gates: a herd of sheep behind a fence off to the left and, across from them, two swings. One was wooden and unoccupied, and I couldn't wait to get out to it.

Hengrave Hall was attended to by a group of people called the Hengrave community. They cooked, cleaned, did laundry, gardened, and performed whatever other tasks a 15th century stone building requires of its keepers. With its collective belief in living simply, the community kept the building cold and dark at night. They turned off the radiators after 8:00 p.m. and kept on only the lights that were absolutely necessary after dark. Guests often would wrap themselves in blankets and grasp flashlights to walk the halls at night.

The days at Hengrave had a different feel. Even the building's corners filled up with light from Hengrave's many windows. I often sat in those windows, on their generous ledges, and drank tea with milk while reading, or journaling, or writing postcards. I remember the first time I looked out and saw the gardens with the bushes cut at an angle that made me feel somewhat unbalanced, and I had to go to my room and grab my coat. The first of many walks began that day. I started in the west gardens, where the flowers smelled like black licorice and a crucifix memorializing the death of Jesus invited quiet. From there, I headed south for a view of the sheep. I had been wanting to get closer ever since I first saw them from the bus window, but I hadn't planned to frighten them witless, which is what I did that first visit. When I approached the fence, they looked curious, like a dog when it cocks its head to one side or lifts up an ear. Then I took one step closer, and they ran a few steps and turned around to face me again, this time wide-eyed and panicked. I moved a bit closer. They ran, stopped, turned around again, looking wider-eyed than before. I hadn't meant to scare them, but soon it was obvious that the sheep were more frightened than ever, bumping wildly into each other. They were running to the back of the fence, scrambling to get as far from me as possible. Whatever game we'd been playing had gone amuck. I'd somehow crossed a boundary, come closer than I'd been welcome, and they were scared, sticking close together, shivering as if I were a lunatic shearer, come to take their skins right along with their wool.

Soon I left the sheep alone, not wanting to overthrow their entire day. I followed the path and came upon that swing I had seen from the bus window. I set down my raincoat to protect my backside from the day's rain and sat down. I began to swing and the higher I reached, the better the view was from above—green in every direction, with the occasional red blur of an apple tree or a snatch of dark blackberries. Then I saw the sheep just ahead, and it seemed they had already forgotten me. They had taken to grazing, chewing on Hengrave grass and keeping away from the fence. They grazed. I swung. We kept busy with our own games.

I stayed on my swing until it started to turn dark, and then I finished my walk through the vegetable gardens, where I picked and ate blackberries; through gates that led to the orchards; on to the south flower gardens; and finally through the same back door I had walked out of two hours earlier.

After our first visit to Hengrave, we resumed our travels. Our trip was structured so that we moved around the entire time, staying in cities—Coventry and Little Gidding and Cambridge and Oxford—for up to four days and then continuing on to a new destination. So we sat on buses, carried our luggage to new hostels, bought maps, tackled layouts of many towns, and then, just as we were getting used to a new place, it was time to leave it behind and move on.

During these weeks, my mind turned often to Hengrave, where I knew the feeling of the mattress below me at night, where the maids stopped in our bedrooms every morning to take away our rubbish and shout at us for not cleaning or returning the mugs we had borrowed from the tea room. At Hengrave I had a place for my shampoo, a corner of the closet that belonged to me alone. I knew that fruit would be served daily after lunch and I could look forward to something more delectable after dinner. I knew the corners of that place like no other we stayed at during our semester abroad.

Hengrave was far from the home I knew on Elm Street back in Minnesota, but I remember the same kinds of details about both of them. From Hengrave I remember the laundry strewn out across the radiators, the braided bread we ate at dinner, the apples I stole from the orchards. I remember washing clothes together, putting our initials on our white underwear so the Hanes-Her-Ways wouldn't get mixed up. I remember wanting to get out on the roof, and even searching there once with my friend Luke, but never making my way to a place that would have given me a view of Hengrave from above. And I remember once going to my swing at night. I took my headset along with me and my raincoat, as it had been raining again. On my way I passed my friend Adam, sitting on the steps and whittling under a tiny light. He had cut himself a few days before, and I watched his fingers work the knife carefully through the wood. He was busy shaping something, shaping anything with the aid of a tiny porch light. I went ahead and set out my coat. It was too dark to see the sheep, and even the trees were only shadows above the swing. I put on my headset, turned on a favorite song about night swimming, and closed my eyes.

I don't remember ever swinging again at Hengrave. I don't even remember details from my last visit. It may have been that I was too busy that last day eating my muesli at breakfast, or packing my Stonehenge mug and school books, or getting the last of my linens to the ladies downstairs. All I know is that, in an instant, we were taking pictures of Alec standing in front of his bus and waving goodbye to the boy with the unruly hair who had planted knobby foreign trees on this land only one week before. And then we were off, clapping for Alec as he took us carefully through the narrow gate one last time.

It's been years since I walked the grounds of Hengrave, ate blackberries from the bramble and played games with the sheep. Since I last felt the grounds of Hengrave beneath my feet I've earned two degrees in writing; spent two and a half years in Asia and another two in a place aptly named Normal, Illinois; married my best friend; given birth to two boys; and landed myself back in Minnesota, where winters chill my bones and summers find me looking out for deer. I'm certain that "my" swing at Hengrave is occupied by someone new these days. Maybe a new generation of sheep has found someone else who frightens them witless. And

Adam, wherever he is, must have found another barely-lit step on which to whittle.

As far away as I am from Hengrave, I'm even further away from Elm Street, where from any direction I could point toward my house and whisper *home*. My map has grown much larger—with streets and building and bodies of water in every direction—and I've been a temporary inhabitant in several places on its surface. Through the decades of my life, my concept of home has morphed many times, but I think I've settled on something like this: Home is a place that challenges us while cradling us; a place that accepts and embraces us while requiring us to keep it well; a place that shapes the edges and cores of our personal landscapes in profound ways. If I hold fast to that definition, then I have to be honest: Home has been a lot of places for me. And like a puzzle, my mapping of place is incomplete. With days ahead of me, there will be more places that will serve as "home."

Even though I wake in Minnesota every morning, I still sometimes find my way back to creeks, where I roll up my pants and wade, looking out for signs of crawfish. And sometimes when I'm awake at night, hungry for wild blackberries, I put on my headset, close my eyes, and play the song about night swimming while looking for the perfect place to lay my raincoat and get a good view of some sheep.

Coming Home

Janet Jerve

After decades wandering
the wilderness alone,

you say to yourself,

I am never telling anyone
where I have been.

And when you do go home
and look in their eyes,

everything has changed.
The rooms are not empty,

their arms are open and
you can see they will listen.

Pain paints across their faces,
We believe you.

Brat

Carol Dunbar

I hit a deer doing fifty on a county road in northern Wisconsin, one unseasonably warm February night. The large side of a furred flank loomed before my windshield; I hit the brakes and our seat belts caught as hooves clattered and put out my headlights. From the backseat my daughter gasped and I swerved to avoid the carcass that bounced off the car. It wasn't uncommon to hit a deer in this part of the country, but in the ten years I had been living here, this was the first time my car had made contact with anything larger than a moth. My reaction surprised me. Instead of pulling over, which I would later reason was the rational thing to do, I kept driving. My car was capable, and so I did what I had always done when confronted with a tough situation.

I kept moving.

When I was a child, my family moved an average of once a year. I was born on the island of Guam, my father a Radioman Second Class in the US Navy. We followed him to California, Florida, Virginia, Portsmouth, Rhode Island, where he was promoted to Lieutenant Commander, and Athens, Georgia, where I was one of two white girls in my class. On the island of Oahu, I took hula in gym class and dated the only "Howlie" in my grade. We lived for the most part on military bases, the housing units divided neatly and painted in Necco wafer colors. As I got older and social situations began to baffle and dominate my life, I noticed a pattern.

Whenever other kids were mean to me because I wore the wrong clothes or said a stupid thing, I told myself, well, this isn't your home for long. You don't belong here. Come April/ November / June, we're going to leave. And we always did.

I never had the experience of belonging to a place. I learned my part, the role of the new girl, and I played it. I mastered the art of making acquaintances, acting impressed, and being told things I didn't and couldn't possibly know. On a surface level, I kept things simple, neat and tidy. We went through our things regularly, weeding out old items we had outgrown, leaving them behind. We didn't paint or plant. My father taught me not to leave marks or holes in my bedroom walls, and after a few hard lessons, I started applying that same wisdom to my friendships. As dedicated as I was to keeping in touch, it never worked out. People forget about you when you're not around. The holes left by the loss of a good friend became too painful to fill, and I developed a tendency to keep to myself. My relationships, like my surroundings, were temporary fixtures, shallow as my bedroom décor.

This behavior carried over into my adult life in uncomfortable ways. For ten years I had been living in the Northland, and yet still I felt like the new girl. Why didn't I belong? This was my home, where my son was born, where I was raising my own family. As an adult, I was a homeowner, a landowner, and yet still, I was uncomfortable. I let other people tell me what it was like to live here, feeling that I couldn't know, didn't know, because of the irreversible fact that I wasn't from anywhere.

As the offspring of a military man, I grew up being called a brat though I never really knew what that meant. I assumed people thought I was snotty because I kept to myself. Turns out, the term BRAT began as an acronym in the British army that stood for *British Regiment Attached Traveler*. That explains a lot to me. The feeling I get whenever I attend local functions is that I'm the one added, the one who wouldn't normally be here, as if I had arrived on the bottom of a boat. We attached travelers are known for our resilience, our tendency to be socially independent, and our ability to live anywhere. But in my mind, being a BRAT meant you don't paint, you don't plant, and you don't put holes in the walls. I was clumsy with relationships, and unskilled at investing in the place where I lived.

As a young mother moving to a new part of the country, one that I had picked and the place that I would stay, my first real home, I wanted to belong. I looked for myself in others. People would ask, "Oh, are you a hunter? Do you ice fish? Garden?" I was the vegetarian daughter of a naval officer who had never planted a bean, and as a new parent, I was much too overwhelmed to tackle new skills. I felt lonely, useless, and unqualified to live out in the wild. I didn't feel like I belonged, and yet, I had decided that this cabin in the north woods of Wisconsin was my new home.

Every place I have ever lived had one thing in common: some folks were nice and others not so nice. It took me a while to realize that my sense of belonging was never really about them. It was a decision that I had to make. Being home should be about being comfortable, and as a BRAT, that sensation has always eluded me. I will forever be grateful to the school janitor who took the time to ask me how I was doing on that night I hit the deer.

My daughter belongs to a wonderful country elementary school eight miles from our house. She aspires to be a marine biologist and is a member of her school's basketball team. The day before we hit the deer, she had set up her first aquarium. A school friend of hers had an overcrowded tank and we were on our way to score our first batch of baby fish when the accident occurred.

As the car hummed through the dark, I tried to read her face in the rear view mirror. It had started to snow, the flakes fat and heavy, splatting on the windshield. From the backseat, my daughter asked,

"Did we kill it?"

"Yes," I said, gripping the wheel. "Yes we did." Of course I didn't know, but certainty seemed best. I could almost hear her brain ticking through scenarios, all of them from the deer's point of view.

"Oh. Oh my gosh."

"I know. I'm sorry. I'm so sorry."

Silence filled the car as I peered through the snow. On her lap she cradled a cardboard box lined with a fleece blanket and a hot water bottle. She had basketball practice that night, and didn't want her new hatchlings to get cold while waiting to be transported home. We arrived at the friend's house and my daughter got out with her box. The friend came running up to meet us, then stopped, gawking at our car.

"All that fur is good!" she exclaimed. "You want to leave that on there so you can take pictures for your insurance."

My daughter and I stared. I had never hit a deer, but apparently everyone else living in northern Wisconsin had. The friend's mom? Oh, she'd hit at least eight. The older daughter who just started driving? She'd hit one last week. Really, it was a miracle I had lived here so long *without* hitting a deer. Welcome to the club, I thought, and I felt a funny kind of twinge.

We left with deer fur dangling from our broken headlight and six baby guppies floating in baggies. We drove to the school where my daughter practiced with her team and I babysat the fish. I paced the library. I didn't know what to do. I thought about calling my husband, calling the sheriff, driving back to get the deer off the road. I had just hung up with 911 when the school's janitor walked into the room.

"Hey!" he said, smiling. "How's it going with you tonight?" He was a tall man with eyes the color of the lake. He always wore sleeveless t-shirts and I liked the way he stopped kids who ran in the halls, even though that wasn't part of his job. The other thing you need to know about the janitor is that one winter afternoon a few years ago, when I had locked my keys in the car, he came out with the school broom and spent half an hour of fiddling to jimmy the lock. I made him cookies to thank him, and we'd kind of been friendly ever since.

"I hit my first deer," I said to him, hanging up the phone. "I'm still kind of shaking."

I held out my hand so he could see. His eyes went large.

"Everybody okay?"

"Everybody but the deer. But yeah, we're fine. We had our seat belts on." He waited and so I described the scene. He was especially interested in the deer, and I remembered then that Mr. Doskey, the janitor, was a hunter.

"How big was it?" he asked, a flash in his eye.

"Oh, he was a giant buck," I said, seeing it all again before me. "I think I saw antlers. His neck was this wide." I showed him with my arms and his eyes got brighter.

"Where did it happen?"

I told him. I also told him he could have the meat. It wasn't the way I had expected the conversation to go, but I was proud of myself for having at least figured out that in this part of the country, it was acceptable to eat your own road kill.

Mr. Doskey did a quick calculation in his head, jingling his keys. He made arrangements, locked the doors, and went off to find our deer.

Ten minutes later, he came back, looked at me, and shook his head laughing.

"What?" I asked, "didn't you find the deer?"

"Yeah, I found him all right. Right where you said."

"And? Was it a buck?"

"No. Just a little thing. A yearling."

"What?"

"And you broke his neck. That's good," he assured me, "It means he didn't suffer none."

"A yearling?" I protested. "Are you sure?"

He smiled, nodded, showed me with his hands.

"No!" I made another motion with my hands, "he was this big!" My arms out wide, we were like a couple of fisherman, arguing about our catch. Mr. Doskey started laughing again, and this time, I joined him.

That night we brought six baby fish home to our new aquarium and watched them explore. They settled in right away, and as the days passed, it became obvious they would thrive. About two weeks later, my husband and I were attending a school function and the janitor stopped our family to ask us if we would like some venison. The little carnivores jumped up and down and I accepted. The following night after basketball practice, Mr. Doskey handed over a neatly wrapped package of frozen steaks with a "To" and "From" inscription written in black sharpie. My daughter ran over and hugged him.

"Thank you," she said, "I love venison."

Mr. Doskey beamed.

"Well, you're welcome. I hope you like it."

I watched my daughter, growing up in the north woods of Wisconsin, not afraid to eat the deer her mother had run over with the minivan. I marveled at her resilience, her good sensibility, and her gratitude. I marveled at the way the three of us could stand there talking, a janitor, a future marine biologist, and a vegetarian who wasn't from around here. For the first time in a long time, I felt comfortable. I realized then that I had been going about this belonging thing all wrong. I didn't need to be like them, and they didn't need to be like me. I belonged because I wanted to be here. And it felt good to be home.

Postcard to Ailene from a Place in the Air

Suzanne Allen

Tonight the moon pulls at my waters and I want to fly away. High above Tuileries on the Ferris wheel—which, from the ground, resembles spinning camembert—this glassed-in gondola turns around and around, ever righting itself with gravity, and one can see how the wind has worn rows of small waves into the garden's dirt path—imperceptible from below, up close. How many seasons shaped them. How much they didn't remind me of you until just now. We left the waves behind, you and I, but keep finding reasons to go back. Ripples in fountains, lapping lakes, rivers coursing past now familiar shores, may never be enough. How bittersweet to go home again and again, righting ourselves and ever leaning towards leaving. How some things are clearer from a distance.

The Ghosts of Abandoned Capacity

David Pichaske

"for there ain't nothin' here now to hold them"
—Bob Dylan, *"North Country Blues"*

These walls hold nothin' neither—
house, apartment, warehouse, barn,
repeat the sad, familiar story:
capacity lost in the modern flight
from home and roots and reality.

The poet pays for his coffee latte
with a Visa credit card,
studies the laptop in front of him,
wouldn't know his boyhood home
if he walked through the living room.

In my Minnesota countryside,
abandoned barns in dense groves
collapse upon themselves.
Plaster cracks in the empty house,
and mice shred the living room sofa.

In Łódź, Poland, the inside walls
of wrecked apartments now face the street:
pastel squares mark kitchen and bath,
framed in squares of grey cement.
The distant echo of childish laughter.

In the rubble, boots and broken toys.
The folks have moved to a beehive bloc,
more convenient to dad's new job.
Home, and the idea of home, are
a cracked cup on the window ledge.

Origins

Andrea Potos

Yaya unwraps the cup
I gave her, its handle molded
into an angel.
She claps her hands like a happy child,
traces the glistening
arcs of its wings
and holds it to her cheek.
Eneh poli ohreho
she cries,
the original words
I cannot translate alone—
they spill through her speech

more and more now,
as if she is letting slip
that knot of English,
leaving the dock where she arrived
seventy years ago streaming back
to that girl in Piraeus,
port of her childhood
where I cannot go,
blue water of her birth.

A Distant Ship Tiding Home

Bruce Pratt

A distant ship tiding home,
reefed against mad easterlies,
tacks north past a bare headland.

Surf swarms a widow's ankles,
sand and prayer surging seaward.
A distant ship tiding home,

heeling in haste to her rail,
chases her salt-flecked bowsprit,
tacks north past a bare headland.

Quarreling east wind and storm tide
roil the gravid sea, savage
a distant ship tiding home,

lash the widow's gathered skirts.
Sails vanished, her harrowed hope
tacks north past a bare headland.

Wind, a murmur of women,
cursing tide, singing shingles.
A distant ship tiding home
tacks north past a bare headland.

DISPLACED PERSON

John Manesis

Unlike other Greek immigrants
with their own businesses,
Nontas never savored
the elixir of success.

They encouraged him
to improve his English skills,
place larger ads in the local paper,
expand the menu of his coffee shop.

This bachelor, private and aloof,
had lived in America forty years
but never felt like he belonged.
He swore he's never return to Greece

and yet he yearned for the village
in the Peloponnesos where he was born.
On many quiet afternoons,
after the waitress had left,

he would stare out the window
and see his father, long deceased,
gesturing beneath an olive tree,
trying to explain to Nontas,

then a boy whose mother had died,
why the youngster would be sent
to live in a place called Fond du Lac

with his childless Thea and Theo.
Beside the glass one day, alone,
he asked his reflection,
"Does it matter anymore?"
Nontas untied his apron,

taped a note on the front door
that read, "closed for good,"
left a ring of keys at the bank
and bought a one way ticket home.

Portrait without Words

Tami Mohamed Brown

My mother-in-law cannot read or write. Married at fourteen, raised to raise a family, she never had the need to spell her name out on paper. In the small village where she grew up, the village she lives in yet today, there are no signs to direct one to the market, the mosque, to the barber shop for men. These are places learned, routes ingrained like the creases and lines that run across the inside of the palm, familiar. Recognizable.

My mother-in-law rarely travels beyond the daily route she has grown accustomed to, a routine she has known since she was a young woman, a routine that still exists in her fifty-fifth year. When she visits her younger sister, ten minutes away in a neighboring village by taxi, she becomes sick and vomits.

Travel is bad for the body, she claims.

The year my husband and I are in Egypt, I rattle back and forth with her in the back of shared taxis on Fridays for this trip each week, playing the role of dutiful daughter-in-law on the five kilometer pilgrimage to the tiny city of Orman. We sit together in the backseat.

Ama, as I call her, wipes the sweat from her face with a tissue, fans herself with both hands, eyes closed. We hit a pothole in the road and scatter a flock of chickens. The small, green leather-bound copy of the Koran is pulled out from under the layers of black and navy blue cloth she is wrapped in. *Bismi'allah a rahem a rameen,* Ama prays under her breath.

I hold on to the door handle, lean my face out the window to catch the breeze, the only motion in the middle of the hot afternoon.

The body shouldn't go too far from home, she tells me and leans closer to wipe the sweat from my forehead. She laughs. Pats my hand.

Travel isn't good for the body, she repeats, choosing simple Arabic words to express this, in case I hadn't understood the first time. There is more wiping, more fanning, the dramatic exhale of breath. She tucks the Koran into my cleavage and pats it into place. We get out of the taxi and she throws up onto the dusty road.

The body shouldn't go too far from home.

My own body has traveled thousands of miles on this journey, across the Atlantic. I am six months pregnant and the Egyptian heat exhausts me, the sun surreal in its brightness against the dun colored buildings that stretch out into the green fields. Most days I cry for no reason. I am constantly ill, tired, dizzy. Ama has an explanation for all my ailments—she believes that everything from fatigue to swollen feet to heat rash is the result of me being out of place.

She says you're too far from home, my husband interprets, as Ama pats my hand, strokes my cheek. And I cry some more.

All around us, in the July heat, houses are being built, cement block arms reaching upwards to support future generations. Ama's house sits flat on the ground. Her daughters have moved into the houses of their husband's families. She has the son in Paris, the son leaving for Saudi Arabia, the son visiting from America with his wife.

I had a dream, Ama tells me almost every morning as we drink our tea. *In my dream, I was very, very old, and this house was the tallest house on the street and you were making breakfast.* She leans close and kisses both my cheeks, and I pretend I don't understand the dream.

When I begin to make arrangements to return to America, she tells me her dreams of airplane crashes and black swamps.

I leave Ama standing with the rest of the family at the taxi stand, where the paved road meets the dirt road that leads out from the village. She is wiping her face with the edges of her scarf and holding a paper package containing a whole cooked chicken, which I've tried to explain for the last week I will not be allowed to take on the airplane.

I travel to Cairo, then on to Amsterdam, to New York, and then finally to Minneapolis, where my husband later joins me, where she refuses to speak to us for months.

America is too far.

The body shouldn't go too far from home, reminds Ama when my husband and I beg her to come to visit us, when we are settled into our American life.

Yes, we agree, it is far. But we can take care of getting the ticket; we can work with Immigration to get the visit visa. We ask her over and over.

Please Ama, I say. *Come see the baby.*

And for years she does not.

But then, when the baby turns six, she changes her mind.

Did you invite Ama to come? I ask my daughter after a long phone call.

I told her I'm never going to Egypt, my daughter replies. *It's too far*.

It is a clear June afternoon when Ama arrives on a huge silver airplane, escorted to International Arrivals by a pilot. She kisses him on both cheeks when he leaves her with us.

She is amazed by how big the baby is, by the gray streak in my hair, by how tired her son looks, here in America for so long.

But most of all, she is amazed by the airplanes.

So big, so beautiful, she says when she sees so many of them dotting the sky from our home near the airport, arching out into the world at angles, so seemingly sure of their destinations.

Airplane, my daughter says to her grandmother. *In English, airplane.*

Tayaura, replies Ama. *En Arabe, Tayaura.*

She sits at the window of our suburban condo and wonders out loud where they are going, so many.

We shout out their imagined destinations: *France! Taiwan! Poland! New York!*

So many, Ama repeats, in Arabic, again and again, shaking her head that we would even begin to guess.

She counts airplanes while we are at work. She counts them from the front seat of our car, which she rides in without becoming ill. She counts them from the park that overlooks the freeway, a point where the planes seem to drop dramatically in their descent, causing her to hold her hand to her heart, to pat the Koran that is carried next to her heart under all of her clothes. She watches the airplanes from the parking lot at the grocery store, from our picnic blanket at the beach.

She explains to the butcher at the middle-eastern grocery how amazing the airplanes are, the sheer numbers that are always flying right over us.

How do they stay up there in the sky? she wonders aloud to him. *It isn't the place for them. So many of them, like big silver birds.*

The butcher smiles. He likes Ama, allows her back in the room where the meat is being cut, lets her boss him around a little. Maybe she reminds him of home.

The airplanes are amazing, he agrees. *But you get used to seeing them. They just become part of the way things are. Routine.*

She kisses him on both cheeks.

One evening, too hot to go outside, we sit at the table and draw pictures, pictures of home, places we know well; the hill that slopes down to the freeway barrier, the lake where we swim, the school playground. We draw places from the imagination, places we have never seen; Saturn and the Great Wall of China, the moon and the sun.

Ama, says my daughter, *if you take off your scarf, I'll draw you.* She looks at her hopefully; she has never seen her grandmother without the scarf covering her head.

Please, she says again in her most convincing voice. *I'll make you so beautiful without your scarf.*

You might not recognize me if I take off my scarf, teases Ama.

I would recognize you! *I recognized you the first time I saw you. Before I knew you.*

She goes back to drawing.

Write my name, Ama says to me.

I write, in Arabic, large, in purple crayon—**Bosaina.**

She studies it, picks up the silver crayon, twirls it between her fingers, laughs at her own awkwardness.

Then she puts the crayon to the paper and presses to make the shapes that mean her name.

The room seems to collapse, to grow smaller as we all watch her, concentrating.

Did Ama really never write before? repeats my daughter in a whisper.

No honey, she really never did, I reply, again and again.

She looks so sad at this, sad for her grandmother. She has made pictures and words since she was small, cannot imagine her world without them.

She smooths the blank paper, clean and fresh and full of possibilities, and slides it across the table to her grandmother.

Look, Ama, you could draw the sun, the moon, she explains. *You could draw a chicken or your house!*

She goes back to her own picture of a girl, with a cat.

Ama hesitates, watching, and begins to draw out the round-belly of an airplane, silver wings. She replaces the silver with blue and makes the blue sky she has been watching for the last month, the planes that have been part of her routine with us.

The picture is simple, but recognizable.

Three Line Bio

Katie Hae Leo

The beautiful boy with rain in his voice
could do it. Put it all into three lines.
Then he would sing it, and pieces
of mystery would suddenly shift,
reveal themselves over guitar strings.
So, too, should the poet be able. Call
up Orpheus, make him do his little jig
for you. Three lines to sum up your life.
Your whole world through your back
window. Grind of the 11 Bus going by.
That hour in the morning when the left
foot of a dream steps into your daylight.
But what they really want is Korea, what
it means to you. Easier to describe wind
down a hallway. How it marries the dark
smell of nighttime, the yellow purr of your
desk lamp. There. There is place in that
and meaning. Those words alone must do.

A Hundred Things

For Mama Josephine, Democratic Republic of Congo

Emily K. Bright

Someone asked me yesterday at work
whether I had ever lived inside a hut and whether
we had grocery stores where I came from?
Pardon me? I asked.
His face was serious as stone.

It will take a year to translate my degree officially,
and then I will hang it on the wall to
stop all the assumptions. Please,
ask me all you wish. The answer is a story.

Listen. What I miss from home
changes with the day, sometimes
spices, turns of phrase.
Being understood. The shadows on the wall
are shorter here; no women carry baskets on their heads.

I used to dream of being in America, but now that I am here,
I am Africa misplaced.
Americans don't feel their muscles coil into ropes each time
a soldier boards the bus. They do not fear
that he has come for them. When their children turn
to gawk, as children do, their eyes hold only fascination.

Long ago I learned to swallow fear and sorrow like great rocks
into my stomach. It is a hungry silence, a necessary crime
to never speak and never scream, no matter

who is killed in front of you.
These memories are woven in my skin.

There are a hundred things to make me long for
anywhere but where I am.
I woke up this morning tasting pumpkin leaves
the way my mother makes them, with onions and a spoonful
of peanut butter for the taste.

Provenance

Nadine Pinede

Where are you from? He asks,
and hands me a wineglass.

Where am I from?

Perhaps the place of my birth,
though all I remember are the scarlet plumes of Bastille Day parades.
Or that town of waist-high snow,
where Peter with the dime-sized freckles calls me nigger
and they ask at school if we stick pins in dolls.

It would be good to know where to scatter my ashes,
where the troubadour dances two-step merengue
with cassava honey hips and the market woman
bears a world on her head, seasons wisdom with proverb
where the ocean roars like a womb, a grave
of teeth and bone, and the whorl of conch shells
blown by runaway slaves called us to battle
where lucky ones hid in the rings of the pine
where fire of dead stars ride time's current
night inside light
where the black sun glows.

Nowhere you'd know, I say
looking down at my glass
and into graying air.

Family Tree

Linda Nemec Foster

There was the rain in the mountains
of southern Poland. Nowy Sacz, the small
town caught in history's time warp: late
1800s and are we in Prussia or Austria?
What country defines this culture
of peasants? My great grandfather,
the only blacksmith in a village
where horses outnumber people.

There was the dense forest
of intense birdsong. My grandfather
straining to understand the language
of dusk. Sparrows, with their dull
gray coats, complaining about the
Old World and its tight shoes.
"Get out, get out," they sing
in unison to the man who gambles
on a one-way ticket to Ellis Island.
Bribes the girl in the next village
to meet him in two years—
underneath the orange sky
above the steel mills of Cleveland.
Say "Cuyahoga," he tells her;
as if it were a river that ran
through her heart.

There was the exotic smell
of india ink on my father's
fingers when he came home
from work. Assembling printing

presses as big as garages, he
forgot the sound of words as
they left the page. He was only
interested in the machine's end
result: capturing letters
on an inked roller's surface.
By the time he died, he'd lost
the language of village and rain.

There was the echo of "I am"—
the confused ego of the immigrant's
granddaughter as she navigates
the New World. She has never
known the language of the Old
and she wants to be nothing
but American. Ageless, classless,
careless. She negotiates a history:
The Compromise of Opposites.
How to immigrate from one world
to another without realizing it.
She leaves her impression, her
empty outline on every major
street in America. Home of the
brave. Last image of an anthem.

There was the unrehearsed
arrival of the son: urban and
urbane. No hint of the rain
in the mountains, the fog
forgetting itself. He knows
only one language and uses
it to reinvent the past. No
history—only now. College
and small rooms. He'll visit
the mountains of Nowy Sacz
once and then instantly
misplace them. A postcard
in the very bottom drawer.

Lands of Song

Joseph Bruchac

My words are stumbling,
but they are trying
Dobry den Slovansky
Oh Land of Songs
three hundred children
taken by the train
to Hungary to never
speak or sing Slovak again,
girls destined to be servants
boys fated to be fitted
with the Hapsburg boots
of soldiers marching
to imperial wars.

Their feet are bleeding
as they try to run,
stumbling over mountains
as the white drifts rise,
barefoot and tired, following
an old melody about
small streams rippling
past a deserted village,
finding the tear-salted sea.

Now I rise to write
these few words by candlelight
on this New Year's morning.

My own blood
shared their flight
to this other shore
where every language,
every ancestor's song
whether Slovak or Indian
was still deemed wrong.

My words are stumbling
like a half-wakened bear
coming down from his cave
in the Tatra Mountains
where the tallest peaks
still hold the snow.

His feet are following
the paths of streams,
freed at last by the thawing.

Grandfathers, Grandmothers,
your way I am walking,
Help me to remember
all of our lost lands,
help me to sing.

III

Living a Second Time in Memory:

Looking Back at Home

Looking Back

Sarah Brown Weitzman

I meant to return long before this
but in looking back we learn too much
of loss and I dreaded that.

Now going through the house
and my parents' lives
too revealed by what they saved

and what they left behind
for me to find, I feel nothing
but pain for the past

trying to understand
how I fell so short of what I intended
to do with my life.

How life twists and turns
against us. How a childhood
is not really understood

until it is lived a second time
in memory. How wonderful
and how terrible

it seems now
because it is gone
and because it was mine.

What Holds Me

Laura L. Hansen

What holds me together is this house
two steps up from the shore of the river,
the closets filled to overflowing
with old rubber boots and overcoats,
with knitted mittens and sleeping bags,
with tents and skates and tennis rackets.
What holds me together is the weight
of the attic with its burden
of ladies' hats and boxes of too-wide ties,
with grandma's teacups and decades
of Christmas cards.
There are cards
from people I remember and names
of people I've never known.
The cards cozy up next to old photos
and report cards and family letters,
curl up on top of wedding albums
and outdated medical texts.
I recently found - rolled in a corner -
the posters that used to decorate my room.
I peered through the two-foot-long tube
as if it was a telescope to the past
and I saw Snoopy dancing and dancing
and dancing through the years
in a swirl of nostalgia and attic dust.
It is dust that holds me here, dust
that cannot be brushed away.
It adheres like a fingerprint taken
and filed, a mark that identifies me
as a prisoner of the past.

The Portable Singer

Penny Perry

before the waking crow and jay chatter
if I were dreaming close to home
I could be roused by another familiar cadence
sounding through the floor wood
the crisp snap of the foot lever
and the start-backup-go of the little black Singer

some of the time it hummed me back to sleep
or the whir was a motor of transport
rarely, I would drag with a child zombie shuffle
down the worn stair treads

to find in the near dark
at the dining room table
my mother, bent over the sewing machine
fenced by the black cord strung to the outlet

her sure hands performed in the close spot of the work light
steering the pinned material under the zipper foot
her right ankle cocked on the footfeed pedal
pressing the pace of experience

most mornings, she was there
early, really early, before work
doing altering jobs for:
J.C. Penney, Spooner Mercantile and Eddy's Dress Shop

from those mere solitary hours
came our Christmas presents
our college books
our example

Fixing Potato Salad While the Past Comes and Goes

Sharon Chmielarz

Mid-August morning at the kitchen counter.
Potatoes and eggs, already boiled.
        My mother peeled them hot.

And her mother and now me. Oh, it looks so easy.
The garden's 260-pound harvest carried in
        to the kitchen, cooked up. One day at a time.

Windows open. Cool breeze. Somewhere down the street
a kid, cranky, hot, bored, crying.
        I'll give you a whop.

Food. A family history of it. Who cut the roast,
who baked, who tried to escape clean-up,
who rolled in the grass after eating too much,
who buttered his refrigerator cookies,
who crashed to the floor in a farmers' cafe,
sausage half chewed in his mouth,
who made something out of nothing,
who had only milk and flour when a child,
in whose house was light craved more than food.

All this in my hands. I mix up the dressing.
Core the green pepper. Dice red onion.
        Did any of them know red onion?

They planted yellow, white and spring green onions,
their gardens' delicacy. One ghost cautions
over my shoulder, "Easy on the onion."

The one who didn't like onion. Hated garlic.
Loved Italian pasta. Go figure. Easy. Easy.
Not too heavy-handed.

The kitchen spins as it does when sun breaks though clouds
and light expands the room into world. Then cloud
cover returns, and I'm looking at a plain, round bowl.

The Hot Corner

John Azrak

I grew up on an intersection in Brooklyn dubbed the hot corner,
drivers in wife-beaters on summer nights screeching onto the avenue,
burning rubber, manhood at stake, beer cans flung at our stoop like Spaldings.
The home in my future would be on Beaver Cleaver's street. At nine,

I saw a man speeding around the corner fly off his motorcycle, helmet-
less head (another *Spaldeen*) bouncing along the curb until his foot caught
in the sewer. When he died in Veteran's Hospital, I ruled out Harley-David-
sons and English racers. Two years later, walking my new Schwinn down

the monster hill past the fortresses of Joey Gallo and Tony Anastasia
(How *did* my working class parents wind up so close to Mafia mansions?)
the garage across from our home exploded, the rooms above on fire.
The baby was lobbed like a softball into the arms of my father. I prayed

out loud and swore off attached garages. After I got sucker-punched
in the school yard for beating a kid in stickball on his turf, I vowed
to send my kids to parochial school, but at fourteen, leaning on the holy water
font after serving 6 am Mass, Father C lifted my ass like a bowling ball

off the rack and I wondered if any home came without a parish. I took
refuge on Dyker Beach golf course, across from our intersection,
but after consecutive birdies (mine), JLM (monogrammed sweater)
sidled up behind me as I washed my ball on the eighth hole and slipped

his gloved hand into my back pocket. I crossed out public links
and imagined the greener fairways of Long Island where I've settled
for three years in a sleepy town with wife and daughter and the itch
to bid on the lone Victorian (detached garage, wraparound porch)

two blocks up from the hot corner.

Homesick

Drew Lamm

Now grown
one candle my fire,
the children scattered as autumn,
the man left long ago.

Lists dangle from my purse,
trail past piles of dirty clothes,
electric bills,
and a dog who wants a walk.

Once I had one room and downstairs
my mother stirring soup,
fresh towels, simple kisses.
When I yawned or cried, I was tucked in.

I write dream parents,
faraway,
please
find me, bring me home.

720 Miles From Home

Ellen Shriner

8:17 a.m. – Eagan, Minnesota

My eight- and five-year-old sons wave goodbye to their father as we drive off. We have a full tank of gas, a sack full of junk food, and the car is still clean. The road trip from the Twin Cities to Toledo has a rhythm all its own. At the one end is my home, where I've created a family, built a business, made a life. The routines that run our household are our own: decaf coffee, National Public Radio, and no meals in front of the TV.

At the other end is the rest of my family: my parents, one sister, two brothers, and their respective families. My history is there. The landmarks bear my French Canadian ancestors' names. Navarre. Cousino. LaPointe. Everywhere I go there's a memory. The high school I attended. The McDonald's where I had my first job. The roads I careened down after the bars closed. The borrow pits where I skinny-dipped on hot August nights. The physical distance is 720 miles. The emotional journey is harder to measure.

I'm the missing puzzle piece, all it takes for the family to be complete. But after more than ten years, I don't quite fit. I have to wedge myself back into the space they've left for me. Sometimes I unsettle other pieces, cause them to shift out of place. Each visit has the potential to be jarring. We discover what's new but remember the shortcomings that are usually obscured by our infrequent visits. Yet I crave these visits. They nurture me.

9:58 a.m. – Highways HH and K, near Eau Claire, Wisconsin

In a state with poetic town names like Eau Claire and Sun Prairie, how did the highway planners convince Wisconsinites to accept the letters of the alphabet as names for their roads? Perhaps the naming system sprang from a wish to tame and impose order on Wisconsin's gently rolling landscape—an impulse like my wish to overlay the messy topography of a week long family visit with the framework of my expectations.

I envision a number of happy vignettes. When I visit my sister, our kids will play together while we have the heart-to-heart talks we've been longing for. Perhaps my oldest brother and I will take my boys to the zoo. He'll like explaining things like why sea anemones wave. My other brother and I will talk business over dinner, sympathizing with each other about maddening clients. When I stay at my parents' house, we'll relax on the screened porch in the deepening dusk while the boys catch fireflies. Too bad our visits don't always unfold the way I'm picturing them.

11:45 a.m. – The Dells, Wisconsin
Billboards touting Tommy Bartlett's water show, the Jellystone campground, and cheese curds beckon. I'm slightly repelled, but also entertained by the exuberant, tacky excess of the Wisconsin Dells. My kids would love it if I'd agree to stop here.

12:45 p.m. – South of Madison, Wisconsin
The mares' tails of western Wisconsin give way to fluffy cumulus clouds, the kind my boys draw. The Holstein-studded pastures and lush green cornfields are monotonous now. I arch my back and shift in my seat to shake off the afternoon lethargy. There's nothing in my head except Mary Chapin Carpenter's "I Feel Lucky" blasting from the radio. I've taken this trip so many times that I know all the times and distances. But still, I want the math to be different. Maybe *this* time, 130 miles will equal something less than two hours.

The timetable of my visits is equally familiar. On the first day, we'll be delighted to see each other. My parents will comment on my new hairstyle and how much the boys have grown. The boys will rush to rediscover the toys my mom keeps for them. We'll look over her flower garden and compare notes on coneflowers and delphinium. My parents will fix my favorite dinner: salmon on the grill, cucumbers in sour cream, and peach pie. I'll revel in being fussed over.

But by the second day, I'll be watching my Dad for signs of irritation as the boys run in and out, slamming the screen door. By the third day, I'll brush aside Mom's advice about using a blanket if the night air is chilly. Around day four, we will have snapped at each other over something silly like how to load the dishwasher. We'll quickly make amends, unwilling to spoil the fifth and last day of the visit.

2:30 P.M. – JANESVILLE, WISCONSIN

The boys doze. Orange Cheeto dust coats their fingers and rings their mouths. Unannounced, construction begins. The orange and white barrels on the left and the black and white stripes on the right narrow my vision to the trailer in front of me.

The way my family interacts is just as restrictive. We're like pinballs—unable to jump the tracks, act differently, and see each other as we really are today. Like most families, we have assigned descriptions: Mom isn't ... Dad is ... I never ... Marty usually ... Margo doesn't ... Dave always ... .

The labels are frequently based on former truths. I want to say, "Wait. That's not me anymore. Nobody else thinks I'm picky. I've learned to be more tolerant." I hate being reminded of my shortcomings, even by people who love me enough to overlook them. But like it or not, I know my basic nature remains, although I've learned to refrain from some of my more tiresome tendencies.

3 P.M. – BELVIDERE OASIS, ILLINOIS

The Illinois toll road rest stops have a bizarre Jetson-like efficiency. The sheer quantity of garbage in and garbage out boggles my mind. Inside, everything feels grimy. The doors have been handled by thousands of people, and probably half of them have just sneezed. The tile floor is greasy and splashed with Coke. The garbage cans overflow. I park my boys at a table with their ice cream cones and head for the restroom. A line of women and squirming girls straggles out the door. I step into line and then back out again, suddenly apprehensive. Leaving the boys alone was very foolish. Anything can happen in Chicagoland. Anywhere, really. I hurry back and find them happily crunching their cones. Instead of being refreshed, I'm harried after the break.

During visits, my siblings and parents often confide their concerns about at least one other family member to me. Each of us has an opinion about what the other person should do—get a better job, stay in the current job, be more tolerant of the kids, deal more firmly with the kids' sassiness, keep a cleaner house, or be less obsessed with schedules and details. By the end of the visit, I feel crisscrossed by secrets and grievances, like Gulliver under the Lilliputians' restraints. Yet, I am pleased by the confidences—they mean I still have a vital role in my family, despite our separation.

3:30 p.m. – Dan Ryan Expressway, Chicago

Greek Orthodox domes and brownstones with bay windows give way to skyscrapers in smog. I love the grit and personality of Chicago, but I hate driving through it. The uncertainty, not the traffic, rattles me, knowing that at any minute I might miss my exit. We plunge into traffic—six lanes in each direction. I take a deep breath and know I won't completely exhale again until Gary, Indiana.

I like my extended family better at a distance. My family, with its complicated allegiances and the undercurrents of frustration, is messy. Every time I visit, we have to adjust to each other's quirks again. It's taxing to be away from my routines and flex to the habits of other households. *What was I thinking?*

Behind me, the boys are fighting. "That Kit Kat bar is mine. You had the last one!"

"No, I didn't! Mom did."

"Mom, he's *eating* it."

Next I hear a quick sharp slap, the thump of a small fist, and a wail.

"You've both lost your treats for fighting. Give me that candy bar. NOW."

A panel truck cuts me off and I brake hard to miss him.

"You two are both in big trouble. Not another word out of either of you for ten minutes."

"But Mom, I didn't do anything. He's the one that ... "

"I DON'T CARE WHO DID WHAT. JUST BE QUIET!"

4:00 p.m. – The Skyway, Chicago

Clapboard duplexes flash by. In the distance, I glimpse blue patches of Lake Michigan. We pass abandoned grain elevators painted like Falstaff beer cans. Several have gaping holes as if King Kong's paw had snatched away a handful of bricks.

The boys are subdued. Their fighting and my shouting are so predictable. So predictable that you'd think I could have avoided my part of it. That's probably as unrealistic as expecting four middle-aged siblings to see eye-to-eye all the time. We are who we are. That we love each other was never in doubt. Truly, there's a lot to like about each of us: Marty's natural curiosity and reluctance to be judgmental, Dave's sense of fun and how involved he is as a father, Margo's generous nature and the way she always believes in me.

4:30 P.M. – GARY, INDIANA

Neat lawns surround square Monopoly-style houses painted in hopeful shades of aqua, orchid, and gold. Driveways with old cars mark off each lot. I try to imagine living there. What work would I do? High school English teacher? Grocery store clerk? Waitress? It looks as if the residents' toehold on the economic ladder is precarious. If you lost your job, would there be another?

Toledo isn't too far removed from this. Like other rustbelt towns, it has limited options. You make do with what's there, or you move away like my husband and I did.

5:45 P.M. – SOUTH BEND, INDIANA

We pull into a Bill Knapp's restaurant for dinner. The food is unremarkable, but at least they'll bring it to you. At the boys' request, we sit three abreast in the booth. My older son tucks himself under my arm. My younger son kneels next to me and buries his face in my hair. They're glad to be back in my good graces.

8/9 P.M. – OHIO LINE

Eastern Daylight Time begins, so I reset my watch. We start to pick up Toledo radio stations and I feel a low hum of excitement. White lines strobe past as we hurtle through Ohio at nearly 80 m.p.h. We've been on the road too long. I feel shocky and unreal. To force myself to slow down, I lift my foot completely off the gas pedal.

10:30 P.M. – MAUMEE/TOLEDO, OHIO

I revel in the familiar landmarks: the farmhouse on Perrysburg Holland Road where my college boyfriend lived, Dana Corp.'s U-Joint division where I sometimes had meetings, the Toledo Clinic where my husband worked, my childhood dentist on Secor Road, and finally, my parents' driveway.

Dad hurries out in his slippers to give me a bear hug. Mom trails behind him with a beaming smile. Blinking at the car's dome light, the boys stumble out of the car and submit to their grandparents' hugs. I become a daughter and a sister again. I am welcomed by people who remember me when I was a shy 13-year-old, a rebellious 19-year-old and who are pleased to see the 43-year-old I've become.

The Avid Heirs of the Farm

Alice Owen Duggan

Every one of us wants the rocking chair by the fire. Of course. And the battered volumes of Dickens dropping shreds of red leather, glass doors that used to protect them, light to read them by. We want the patience around our grandmother's mouth, and the sidelong look she gave to things, so she wouldn't have to see them so baldly. Even to heaven she gave a sidelong look. And the harsh scrape of shovels in the barn, the clank of milk cans dropped into the cooler. The heat and strength of the men. Our uncles. The way they laughed, the booming delight. The fights. We, the avid heirs of the farm, all want that hearth and its warm ashes. When we go to bed at night we know: Gone. Razed. Flattened to nothing. Still we dream: We will go back with crowbars, pry up the floorboards. There will be more.

Paradise Lost

Jan Chronister

Leaving the homestead
left behind cheap linoleum
ancient isinglass stove
babies bathed in kerosene glow
evangelists preaching paradise
on a cheap transistor radio.
No store-bought diapers
or washing machine
an Eden without
electricity.

Fresh hay
scented quiet nights.
We milked goats
pumped water
polished chimneys on Aladdin lamps.

Last year they bulldozed down the house,
no more rubbing, no more wishes.

Former Tenants

Dan Campion

The vacant lot fills with snow.
Last summer saw our old house torn
to laths and plaster, choking haze,
its frame a tangle, wires frayed,
the mildewed roof and chimney spent
a hundred years from being raised.
Winter's landlord now. Tenantless,
warped shingle siding tumbled down
I painted once in lieu of rent,
those stifling, tentlike attic rooms
are blurry prisms wind collects
for auction like unclaimed effects.
That kitchen where the pipes could freeze
while bread was baking finally glows,
redone, in pristine ice, at last.
Here miles away, flakes coarse as ash
unfold their message wrapped in smoke
that burns against the window glass.

Porch Light

J. Patrick Lewis

After the cat curls round the pump,
and the heat of the day is pulled away
by semis streaming west, after the corn
stalks bow, whispering stories to moles
beside their tunnels, after the screech
owls swivel into place to guard the sky
against the cicadas' horror music
and the sizzling crickets, I am what
you will come home to, you barn-bound
boys scooping up the trifles of your lives,
racing past your childhoods into brown
haze, mysteriously, the color of the future.

Back in Your Old House in Montana

Judith Waller Carroll

Back in your old house in Montana,
your mother hums something by Sinatra.
Outside, piles of leaves circle the yard
like teepees. Soon she will go out
to burn them, squinting against the smoke.
But there is a fire in the stove
so she lingers a while, sipping her coffee.

What you would give to go back
to that time and sit down beside her.
All day, the name of the tune she was humming
purrs around the edge of your memory
like a cat around your ankles, then glides away
just as you reach out to hold it.

The Meaning of Things

Claudia M. Reder

First it was her purses she wondered about, then
the silver soup spoons, then back to purses; one day, out of the blue—
her umbrellas—as if having them back again
would give meaning to her life—
which was a wheel chair life—her words.

Her anxiety grows, *Who put these things in this room,*
the one I live in now? implying, "How did I get here.
Tell me again, how it happened, the stroke."

And I would tell again how it happened,
how we moved her and by phone she told us
what she wanted and didn't want;
how my sister and I had to form choices,
how we didn't think she'd need umbrellas;
how we gave away her stylish clothes.

Well, she says, *At least we didn't put everything in a dumpster*
like another family she knows. Losing control,
she wants to know *Where are my things,*
by this she means my life that rides on the flotsam
and jetsam of accidents and emergencies.

Here you are mother, here, in this chair, here are your arms, mother,
push, push. Let the past go. *I have only one regret,*
she says, but meanwhile, *Where are my things?*

The Heart of the Matter

Karen Herseth Wee

This house
raised against all odds
on the east side of Sand Lake
in South Dakota 1908
rebuilt itself
in my heart

In the years
after I was twenty
I moved fast
moved eight different
times in fewer years
unaware of builders
already contracted and at work
on a monumental task
in my heart's space—
oak banisters and all

Seventeen
individually-carved dowels
to the landing
Twenty-seven more
to the second floor
The ground floor pillar
had a loose top
where a kid dropped
our German oak
nutcracker one holiday

We didn't tell—
he lay there years
I searched
with a flashlight
but he was gone
I do not know his rescuer

No other truly
grand houses line
Sand Lake the kind
with carved lintels
above each downstairs window
and sliding oak doors
between living
and dining room
But even such a house
could not save
Grandmother Herseth
from her own dark interior
as Grandpa Lars' large
laugh resounded
through its rooms
after he'd bet on horses
or drunk himself into stupors
in distant towns

This house's
attic in my heart
allows such a view
of distance
that to this day
hills or too many
tall trees closet me

A refinished bookcase
held cattle medicine
in my young dad-helping days
The dining room still contains
the carved table
buffet and eight chairs
my mother bought
for seventy-four eighty-eight
when she was very young
before her marriage even

My luck—
to be brought
to this house in 1940
a newborn
I know its intimacies
every depth of corner
I can move in its dark
without sound
my hand finding
light switches or exits
before my head does

Each spring
the pull on my body
home
foreshadows
the day
my heart falls down—
the great grandfather
clock finally quiet
in the heart's room

The women who come
to this house to live
with the men who own it
do not know their way here
as my sister and I do
and banished we
resent those
who later
offer civilly
to please feel at home

All the rest of their years
that they live
in this house
they will never carry
its great weight
in such a small place
as a heart

Pecans

Connie Wanek

The travelers brought us pecans from Las Cruces
and I saw again the place I lived so long,
where the Rio Grande flows wide and shallow.
I saw my father with his eyes closed
basking in the early sun
sipping a cup of strong black coffee.
I saw my mother pacing the dry yard, planning
the pear and apple trees she'd grown up north
that suffered so during desert summers.
I stood again at the kitchen sink, looking out,
my hands idle in the dish water,
and watched a vagrant stoop in the back alley
to fill his pockets with fallen pecans.
He was passing through, heading for the coast,
guided by instinct like waterfowl.
Why we must go we can't say.
Some blame the heavens, the restless stars,
some the earth, spinning under our feet
like a ball under an acrobat.

In the palm pecans resemble a clutch of wild eggs,
brown and oblong, full of blueprints.
The trees themselves were the pride of the yard;
their green shelter and the scent of their shade
reminded mother of her Wisconsin.
When we walked beneath them in late fall
we stepped on pecans, and they cracked
against the dry earth. Sometimes we all pitched in

to pick them up, all the sisters and brothers,
working under threat of punishment, or cajoled with bribes.
In those days we owned a black border collie
that ran away every night
with every intention of coming home,
though one night she finally didn't.
I wonder at those
who stay in the same place their whole lives;
I wonder where I'll die.
At some point we just want what's easiest.

Pecans are not native to Las Cruces;
they need far more rain than falls in the desert.
But water flows all summer from the river,
diverted through long muddy ditches
and the trough of the valley
fills with greenery and bees. A place is both itself
and what we make of it, as we are ourselves
and what a place makes of us.
No Waneks at all are left in that town.

The travelers brought pecans, coarse and rustic,
the husk still attached to one or two,
here a bark fragment, a blade of blonde grass.
I was glad to see them.
Only one pecan in perhaps a million sends out roots,
a sturdy green shoot,
and by some accidental or deliberate circumstance
becomes the tree that blooms and bears
year after year in the same soil.
The rest of the pecans are organized and eaten.
If this is sad, tell me what is not sad.

Land

Judith Prest

who will know this land
when we are gone?
cardinals stitching scarlet paths
through the brush
wood thrush and Carolina wrens calling
the flight of glossy ibis
heading toward the river

clouds of blackbirds
        rushing to roost before dark:
a percussion of wings, making their own wind
crackling calls filling up the sky

who will know
where to gather crows-foot for wreaths,
the secret places of club moss and pine

when we are gone
who will recall
the sweetness
of the first spring peepers
drifting uphill from the railroad ditch

the lazy brown of the creek
in July's thick heat
where I see my own shadow,
        a toddler in the garden
        biting into a warm tomato
        juice running down my chin,
all of it in front of me,
all of it in my hand then

IV

Seeking Shelter:

Without a Place to Call Home

Dear God of H________

Ethna McKiernan

Oh God of the trumpet red sunrise
burning through the tarp above my tent;
dear God of the warming jeans on the clothesline
hooked between two trees,
God of Dan's sleeping form, let him wake
and light the fire for coffee, let him not
be too hungover from dreams of Gulf War fires
or from vodka; let peace roll over our small camp
as it deserves to roll.

Lord of Shelterdom, I've been to your floor mats
on Currie Avenue, I've watched
more crack pipes brighten up the street
than the bored security officers have seen;
I've had my shoes stripped from me in the night
and have been punched when brushing past another man's mat
while getting up to use the john. Lord, I've entered
your chapel of the Salvation Army and felt no salvation there
where I've almost spit, God, on *you*, my God on you.

Yaweh of joblessness, when the plant closed
the kids and I became a rudderless boat
careening through deepening waves.
Jonah hates the "shelterbus" ride to school; Jane's too young
to know. Today I walked to Welfare to complete more forms,
then to a market two miles away for dinner things, then
to the diabetes clinic for my check-up. My feet burn,
my toes are fat cows. Holiness, I have no busfare.

Rain down, oh rain down, you desolate
blessed God of homelessness.
You with your large hands,
play it out: bestow on us every clement bit of justice
that you own, for today is a day tender as April,
and it carries the shudder of goodness.

Chicken Charlie

Fran Markover

His cardboard box seemed cozy,
flannel shirts doubling as pillow,
vodka bottle a moonlit candle.
Sometimes I'd slip him day old rolls
from Albert's where I sold bread.
My junior high friends and I played
guessing games. What was the length
of his beard, the origin of his name.
Had he lived on a farm like mine?
Although my parents had warned
never talk to strangers, the night
of the Christmas pageant, I walked
toward the church, my choir robe
floating like a sail into chilly wind.
I peeked into his home, could see
the clouds our breath made, his grin
as he whispered *Angel.*

Expired Stars

for Gary DeCramer

Laura Jean

We live underground in this small two bedroom apartment. Our door is tucked under at the mouth of a cavernous stairwell. It's the edge of a black hole. The light at the opening is a halo pulled into the darkness. The old guy slips in before 10 p.m. when the doors are locked; we pretend we don't know he is there. Everything he owns is under there—a small makeshift bed and a little table made from a box with a tattered paperback on it.

It is the end of summer, and as the weather shifts, my subterranean plaster walls feel colder. My small purple metal bed sits in the corner of our tiny burrow. I am tucked in under my Raggedy Ann bedspread. My teddy bears in makeshift jumpers from my butterfly underwear, line the edge of my bed. All except for Chubby, who is firmly tucked under my arm. This soft white bear has blue eyes and an ear the manufacturer sewed on backwards.

By the time we go in the morning the guy is gone for the day. Once I caught a glimpse of him heading out, his hair mostly grey, wearing a plaid shirt and jeans. Later he brought me stuffed toys that he had rescued from the dumpsters that lined the backside of our block. A bear that was purple and gold and a little dirty. I didn't understand why I couldn't keep it.

You could find great things in the dumpsters at the end of a month. We kids would acquire entire living rooms, dragging our new furniture across the asphalt parking lots to a cove of pines where we'd make a fort. On a Saturday afternoon the world could be whatever we imagined. We were warned not to play in or around the dumpsters, but who could resist such unknown possible treasures.

At dusk we play hide and seek. I'm only allowed to stay out because the older girls are out too. As the last of the light disappears from the sky we come in rattling down the stairs. Reaching for my doorknob I can hear the soft, deep breathing of the guy in the black hole. He is sleeping. Weeks go by, until one day the caretaker who lives on the third floor discovers his things and tosses the bundle into the dumpster.

For a time the hole is ours again and we kids are lured in by its gravitational pull. We play under there with flashlights, cautiously hunting out the dust bunnies. Exhilarated, we are afraid of what cannot be seen. There I find a color photograph, its rounded corner bent on one side. It is the guy with his family, a wife and two kids. He looks younger and they look happy. There is no writing on the back, only dust. Gently brushing it off I leave it, hopeful he will come back looking for what was lost.

Lying in my bed, I think about the guy under the stairs, wandering the world alone, and wonder if his story was like my great uncle Walter. He was my grandmother's uncle who served in the First World War. Walter was married and had two boys. He used to disappear and go out riding the rails. I picture him asleep in a still boxcar, the stars radiating, the crickets humming. One day he said was going to join the Merchant Marines and no one ever heard from him again. Aunt Pearl had to wait seven years before she could declare him dead. I have his picture on my staircase wall with his mother, two sisters, and a brother, a well-dressed working class family. I imagine him building forts as a boy, his mother coddling him as the youngest, the baby, tucking him at night.

When we go to the park I look for places one could hide if they didn't have a home, places that would keep you dry and out of the wind, places you could stretch your legs and sleep. I think of the guy and Uncle Walter finding places to sleep along the rails, hidden spaces under bridges, and stairwells, expired stars that have collapsed in darkness.

A Shelter Is Not a Home

Linda Kantner

A shelter is not a home. It's a place to go when there is no place else. It's a place to be, not a place to live. A shelter for children is a place to wait. Wait until somebody decides you can live in a home again. Your home, a foster home, a group home. Wait until your family is fit or you're able to fit into someone else's home. Wait until you or your family recognize that how you have been living is not what everyone else thinks is normal. Wait until everyone changes. Wait and wait and wait.

Wait because your mother drinks too much and forgets to come home. Or she takes you to the bar and makes you wait in the car. It gets cold and your fingers freeze. She forgets to buy food or send you to school. She forgets that she is smoking and burns long black scars into the couch and the kitchen table and her sheets. You watch her and you put out the fires just in time. Sometimes you watch her all night. Now that you're in the shelter who watches her? Who will put out the fires? Who reminds her that you exist?

Wait because your dad put his hands in your underpants every Friday night while your mom was at work. You learned at school that this was not okay. You told your mom about it and she said don't make up such nasty things. So you told your teacher even though your dad and mom both told you not to. Now everybody is mad at you and you can't go home.

Wait because your mom goes crazy sometimes. She sees the walls bleed. She needs you to stay at home and mop up the blood. She forgets to take her medicine or decides not to take it because it's poison. Then she thinks you are the wicked and she hangs you out of the apartment window by your feet. You live on the third floor and she hopes to scare the devil out of you. You think maybe she has.

Wait because your dad believes in hitting. He believes in respect and fear. He believes in the wooden spoon and wire coat hangers and black leather belts. He believes in his fist. He wouldn't hit you if you weren't so bad. He wishes to God he didn't have to. So do you.

You wait in the shelter with kids who are so mean. They say "fuck" all the time and hit for no reason. They call your mamma a whore, a bitch and a slut. If you ever get anything new like tennis shoes from the social worker they steal 'em or rip 'em or throw 'em on the roof.

If the kids aren't mean then they're crazy. They giggle for no reason or pull down their pants in the lunch room or shit on the floor. If the staff asks why they did that, they just laugh or twirl or bump their heads against the wall. They make you nervous and sometimes they make you laugh. Most of the time you just hope you don't end up like them.

The worst kids are the criers. They cry when they come in and they never quit. If you touch them they cry, if you look at them they cry. If you don't look at them they cry too. All they say is, "I want to go home. Please, let me go home." It reminds you that you're not home and you want to hit them. But if you punch them the staff says, "You better not do that. No family is going to want a kid who hits."

That list goes on forever. No family wants a kid who swears, who wets the bed, who leaves their clothes on the floor, who picks their nose, who is fat, who doesn't do homework. No one wants a kid who is afraid of the dark, who lights fires, who runs from school, who is dumb, whose dad stuck his hands in their underpants.

No family wants the kind of kid who waits in the shelter. Waits behind walls made of concrete blocks painted the color of snot. Walls carved with initials and dirty words and "mom." That word is crossed out, painted over, put in a heart, burnt with matches. Rooms lit by a flash of fluorescent that makes a kid look like a raw plucked chicken. The rooms smell like the given up, given away, hand me down stench of the Goodwill Store. Beds are bolted to the wall. The mattresses are made of loud cold plastic that cracks when you lie on it, giving away every secret bedtime move that could comfort you.

"Don't touch yourself." The staff yells from the front desk giving away what you're doing. "No one wants a kid who does that."

Then one day the social worker calls out your name. He says, "Get your stuff, they have found a family for you." You fall onto the mud colored carpet like you have been shot. You throw your arms and legs around the social worker's steel desk and scream, "No, I don't want to go. Please don't make me go. I want to stay here. I'll do anything. I'll be good."

Suddenly you love the green Jell-o filled with peas and red pimento that they serve every Tuesday. Your room with no door knob and ten boxes of Fruit Loops hidden under the bed is the coziest place you have ever stayed. The kid who smashed the ceramic owl you were making for your mom is your best friend. The staff lady who embarrasses you also tucks you in every night. She says, "Sleep well, pleasant dreams." She's there when you wake up screaming and she'll let you listen to the all-night gospel review on the radio until it is safe enough to go back to bed.

The social worker says, "You can't stay here. This is no place for a kid to grow up."

But it's too late. You already have grown up. You were grown up before you came. The Shelter is a break from being grown up. It's safe here. If you were to run away this is where you would run. This is home for a kid who hits and steals and swears too much. This is home to a booger eater and bed wetter and a crazy kid. The Shelter is home for a kid whose father put his hands in her underpants every Friday night.

The shelter is home.

A Teacher Mourns Disappearance

Julie Landsman

Light falls across a room,
glass bird on a shelf
catches sunshine in early evening,
or breakfast smells come up the same old stairs:
these form the seasons of a home.
A girl finds refuge in dependable light after a tough day
on the playground, or after getting off the bus
on the corner of Lake Street and 14th when the boy
with the red shirt teases her about her skinny legs.

Yet in my room kids breathe in quick-step,
stutter into my class arm and arm with anxiety.
Ten-year-old Lee, whose mother works the night shift,
arrives in the same impeccable blouse each day.
She has taken her baby brother to the neighbor's,
carrying Justin on one thin hip from the Shelter
to the old woman with too many cats.

I create order out of chaos for the few hours
I have them with me, the few months they live in my neighborhood.
If I can touch their shoulder, nudge them awake as they
drift off some afternoons, after a night
trudging to a new bed, clothes in a pillow case
bumping against their knees, wanting only somewhere
soft, I can give them a season. Perhaps the slant of
sun beams changing from March to April on my bookshelf
will hold them. Sadie comes early, bustles to help me assemble

crayons, paper, scissors, while Troy
dances through the doorway 8th week in a row,
still home, still here. We silently bless consecutive days, turn
toward the board and begin our work:
how to tell time
how to predict the weather,
how to measure rainfall.

I hold my breath until they are before me each morning:
drifting kids;
city nomads.

I relax when they appear for at least one more
day of snow against my window.

I sleep easy until
Sadie disappears.
Somewhere she claims one corner
of one room for
her consistent stuffed dog,
her red diary book.
I lose hope when
Troy does not twirl
through the door,
on a Monday after spring vacation.

My classroom is bereft of his song.

I imagine him, over on the North side of the city,
trying to get used to the way the season changes
in a windowless school, bending over a book
under fluorescent light, a new teacher laying her hand
gently on his shoulder, asking him his name.

The Horror of the World Around

Freya Manfred

If you have no warm room
where you can sit and stare into a tea cup,
if no grim women divorced from their bodies
arrive at your door with underarm Bibles, crooning,
"Are you longing for a power
greater and wiser than yourself?",
if no one leaves notes on your windshield saying,
"We'll take this Chevy off your hands for a hundred,"
then you are left
with the horror of the world around.
You are at war, marching into enemy territory,
taking lives or letting your life be taken.
Women stand at their back doors
and avert their eyes from you.
Every town looks the same:
freeways, truck stops, no trespassing.
You're lucky to find a cave in a large tree
where you can crouch when it rains,
or a refrigerator box
where you can cut a small hole and peer out
like when you were a child in your own back yard,
and at sunset, mother called you home.

Passing Through? Squatting is Another Name for Home

Jessica Erica Hahn

Squatting has always fascinated me—the act of taking an empty place and making it a home, albeit temporary. Abandoned buildings are puzzling entities whose owners have disappeared into some misty bureaucratic jungle, a Bermuda Triangle of financial or physical hardship. It can be argued history is a series of episodes of people claiming ownership through force. The concept of adverse possession means, essentially, that if you squat an un-occupied place long enough, you may own the place.

When Americans were frenzied with Western expansion and Manifest Destiny, the government encouraged citizens to settle whatever unclaimed land tickled their fancy. The Preemption Act of 1841 encouraged men over twenty-one and widows to find up to 160 acres, squat it for awhile, and purchase it for as paltry a sum as $1.25 an acre before the land was publically auctioned. Congress knew people were invariably going to squat this vast country, so they devised this Act to make squatters pay. On May 20th, 1862 Abraham Lincoln's signature put the Homestead Act into effect, similar to the Preemption Act, but granting land ownership to freed slaves, immigrants intent on citizenship, and anyone who'd never taken up arms against the government. All one had to do was squat some acreage for five years and pay a nominal filing fee. There were thousands upon thousands of homesteaders by the end of the nineteenth century. One might say squatters founded our country.

Kids of the Black Hole

Some say squatting is a crime, a conflict between owner and occupier, but it's an urban lifestyle, movement in an alternative economy, life under the radar. I associate squatting with Punk culture. In the 1990s, when I was 15 to 25, Punk philosophy was radically appealing, its participants against monoculture, sexism, gentrification, the military-industrial complex, and a money-based economy. The Adolescents sang about "the kids of the black hole" who lived in a "house that belonged to all the homeless kids." Punks believed in direct action, whereas academics talked about change. Squatting was subversive, isolated from mainstream society, a "fuck you" to the structure of renting and working, and viable—think of the Lower East Side with its reclaimed abandoned buildings that house hundreds of people, or Christiania in Copenhagen, an autonomous "freetown" of thousands since the early 1970s. People could live free? *Really?*

An abandoned house is useless without people—people create homes, bring them to life, define them by existing within. Laws regarding trespassing and property interpretation vary; apathetic owners, undisturbed neighbors, and dedicated dwellers kept squats alive. Cultural theorist Michel de Certeau wrote about "ordinary practitioners of the city... they are walkers, *Wandersmanner*, whose bodies follow the thicks and thins of an urban 'text' they write without being able to read it. These practitioners make use of spaces that cannot be seen." Punks embrace the ugly spaces with CAUTION tape hung out front, and like urban warriors, fight for use of those spaces.

Not only did Punks live free, but they espoused feminist ideology. Punk women embodied the antithesis of the standard of beauty, and Punk's lyrical equality was impressive. (Poly Styrene, the teenage singer of X-Ray Spexs, hollered "Some people think that little girls should be seen and not heard, but I say oh bondage, up yours!" while Eve Libertine of Crass sang about unappealing women who were "sweet, defenseless, golden-eyed, a gift of god's repression") According to Craig O'Hara in *The Philosophy of Punk*, "There is no denying sexism exists within the Punk community, but it is on a smaller level than in the mainstream, and more importantly, it is discouraged and condemned by many active participants." Squatting wasn't gender biased—anyone could make a home, *and* travel. The Pogues's version of "Waltzing Matilda" played in my mind: "When I was a young man I carried my pack / And I lived the free life of a rover." If some boy could do it, well *so could I.*

Travelers in an Antique Land

For all the might and money behind Las Vegas and its affronting structures in a desert land, its black pyramid and golden Trump tower are doomed, one day. The image of its demise is beautiful and emotional, a jolt into time travel, like "Ozymandias" by Percy Bysshe Shelley: "...*Two vast and trunkless legs of stone / Stand in the desert... Round the decay / Of that colossal wreck, boundless and bare, / The lone and level sands stretch far away...*"

Quick as ivy, Mother Nature stakes her claim over human endeavors at immortality—see the grassy WWII autobahns in Poland, the rusty rollercoaster tracks of Takakanonuma Park in Japan, and Sutro Baths in San Francisco where vast glass swimming pools perched on the edge of the sea. Ozymandias's shadow lingers in Detroit among buildings where wood carved in filigree shapes and painted ceilings in cavernous lobbies once dazzled eyes long dead. Who is so proud to think he owns a building forever?

In the late 1800s, the Gold Medal Flour factory of the Twin Cities milled enough flour for twelve million loaves of bread a day, until a spark ignited flour dust. When I slept there, it was an eerie wreck of high grey walls and exposed staircases. Dust became paste when it rained, but despite the filth I had tender, lovely moments. If anyone thinks it's not romantic to stargaze on a balmy summer night from a rooftop vantage point, surrounded by rubble and nobody but you and yours, then they don't know romance.

My squats have been in homes, a mansion, a clinic (with grisly patient files that turned my stomach), and drafty warehouses. The spectrum ranges from a jewel box in the Haight-Ashbury to a soggy theater in New Orleans where fliers for a performance by Grace Jones lay alongside the shellacked head of a baby alligator. A printing press in Portland had running water, electricity, and a treasure chest of wooden racks with antique type. (If not bent on traveling lightly, I'd have filled my pockets with the alphabet.) Friends have made homes in missile silos, subway tunnels, churches, hospitals, railway depots, under and inside bridges, and in neighborhoods turned ghost town. I've mostly made my illegal bed in the United States on mushy carpets, wood planks, and sheets of cardboard, but also on concrete slabs in Germany and Switzerland, where a wrecking ball woke me. Under sighing roofs, rustling pigeons, and chewing termites, Ozymandias grins and Janis Joplin reminds, "Get it while you can."

Logistics

On a logistical level, squatting had some intense aspects for my gender. During my period, I wanted water for washing, and safety-pinned socks into my underwear. I said, "When I have a baby I'll take it train hopping!" or some such, but I feared pregnancy. I never wanted to be a man, just a woman living stealthily and walking confidently.

My first task after opening a squat was exploration, then security (locks or barricades), and then checking for functional amenities. Creating a sense of home was a psychological necessity, entailing stockpiling food, schlepping in scavenged furniture, and making a place safe to cook, kick back, have sex, and remove my socks.

On a world level, squats are about subsistence. Miles of shantytowns ringed the old Bombay I saw as a twelve-year-old traveling with my hippie mother. Robert Neuwirth, author of *Shadow Cities*, describes Brazilian "squatter villages" of "150,000 people strong"—I've never experienced living in such an environment. Poverty in America isn't poverty in Ghana, and squats of the first world seem luxurious.

City by the Bay

My ex-boyfriend, Dan, and I scoped out a house on Shotwell Street in San Francisco, an Italianate Victorian, dilapidated from a century of use and abuse, tall and narrow, elegantly composed with bay windows, balustrades, decorations in the trim, grand as the magnolia out front. What fool bequeathed this to rats and weevils? We hopped the cyclone fence, ventured through foxtails and fennel, and jimmied a window with a crowbar.

We changed locks and duplicated the keys on Mission Street. A neighbor happened to volunteer at Food Not Bombs and he lugged over a bucket of water daily to flush our otherwise broken toilet. Six of us lived in the house, using candles for light, cooking on Sternos, growing fraternal, occasionally argumentative. It was a home, no doubt about it. Now fifteen years later, an austere apartment building has taken its place.

Live Free, NYC

Squats in Manhattan were different from those in California: New Yorkers had mad love, fierce pride, and a sense of ownership. Their squats were filled with people of all nationalities and artistic temperaments, living under one roof in a money-free economy, equipped with conveniences like electricity and plumbing, wrestled from the city. They felt militant, and justifiably so—these New Yorkers were organized community members who used terms like "adverse possession," and some were parents with children. One couldn't just sashay inside; like any castle worth it's keep, one earned entrance.

Mayor Giuliani cracked down on the people who embodied the motto "live free," creating a war zone in the name of home ownership. In 1999, Michael Cooper of *The New York Times* described one scene: "As a police helicopter circled overhead, officers from the Emergency Service Unit wearing white sanitary-protection suits struggled to break through barricades at the front of the six-story tenement at 713 East Ninth Street, where squatters had fortified themselves behind new concrete block walls reinforced with steel." It would be terrible to lose what those homesteaders stood for, the power of the people.

Conclusion

Each squat is a home but also a testament to a past, a mortgage gone belly up, two wires crossed in a way that starts a conflagration. Every staircase, hallway and attic is part of the poetry defining home, the painting of alleys and brown lawns, the music of insects. Lingering bronchial issues are my regret—did the particleboard rain asbestos dust while I slept?

Now in my thirties, I'm a mother and homeowner. The room in which I typed this essay was a square of dirt in an oft-ignored neighborhood of San Francisco, Visitacion Valley, but negotiating with the planning department, I picked up a hammer. I hope to teach my daughter cooperative values and survival skills like those New Yorker squatter parents taught their young, even if she grows up in a home owned by the bank.

There is something to be learned from the squatter ideology—part Ozymandias, part hardhat—something poetic yet practical. Eye and brain notice abandoned buildings everywhere, body reacts, brain whirs. This city is a body, and these homes are all of ours as we walk, negotiate pathways, create spaces.

Who really owns the land? We are a funny breed, we humans. We die and pass it on in a succession for posterity. We hope we're so important, writing our memoirs or polemical tracts, but in the advent of global warming life might devolve to a far more subsistent, hand-to-mouth venture. My partner is a person of science who believes if the nuclear bombs went off and all humans died, only the oceans, lower forms of life, and land would remain. Eventually plants and animals come back. Trees grow, roots deepen, streams change course, and muscles build homes. We kill for land we think we own. In reality we are passing through on a temporary basis. In the meantime we are caretakers.

The Cul-de-sac on Tallman Circle

Roberta J. Hill

I drive up and down the silent, empty streets
With bungalows, neat and radiant as dominoes
Lined up on a table in the sun. The one who
Owns 5791 answers when I ring.
"For Sale" goes swinging
In March wind. God is good. People on this side
Do not hang out on their stoops. They're solid
As plum jam in times of war.

She scans my old car, my purse clutched under
My arm, my brown face, outrageous hair, eyes tired
From driving there. She doesn't ask me in,
Doesn't want my name, won't ask about my dream
To live on this seamless side, the proper side
I was told, where whatever happened
Happened here. So, am I out or in?
Beige drapes block my view.
The asking price grows ten grand.

Forshocks

M. J. Fievre

Some things have not changed—the crunchy gravel of the dirt roads, the rooster's crow, the buzz of bees, the bright yellow sun of the Haitian dawn. The rest is spooky in its familiarity, yet wrong in detail. A chill settles over me. Even my skin has gone cold. I drive holding the steering wheel close, among the crowds of unwashed and bewildered faces, the makeshift tent villages. Sometimes, a humanitarian truck comes barreling up behind me and rides my tailpipe.

In Turgeau, where rubble still blocks many streets, I slow down to look for recognizable landmarks. That's probably the time when I should blame God, wonder if He got angry for being mocked, if His patience simply ran out—the moment when I should decide that He probably sees us all, unblinking. But I can't stop believing in His love and I am angry for this faith that I carry around like excess baggage.

As I park the car on Jean Paul II Avenue, I remember la Fête Dieu. In my childhood, many streets in Turgeau would be closed to traffic so that devoted Christians could assemble the magnificent carpets, meticulously made of flower petals, pine needles, and palm fronds. At six o'clock in the morning, a procession of Roman soldiers mouthing sorrowful songs, and of purple-robed penitents carrying a statue of Jesus on the cross, paraded in front of the houses, destroying the carpets, a great honor for those who worked all night creating them. One year, as a teenager, I took part in the procession and fell in love with one of the boy soldiers. That day, I beseeched God to allow me to marry a good man, a non-violent man, different from my father, so I could walk down the aisle of Sacré Coeur in a billowy white dress.

Now my city is lost, the ground covered in dusty, dry blood.

The burning sun toasts my body. I stand across the street from what used to be Dynamic Club, the place where I exercised during my only two years as a med student. At the time, all I knew about health was how to stabilize a broken limb or broken neck and bandage a sprain. I could do mouth-to-mouth and a bit of CPR. I barely knew how to find a vein or administer a drip. At lunch time, I drove to Dynamic Club with Estelle to lift weights and run on the treadmill. I drove my first car around Turgeau, a red Isuzu Trooper that did not always stop when you pushed the brakes.

It was in front of Dynamic Club one day that I noticed the small bullet hole in the rear window of the Isuzu. A silver filigree of cracks ran from the edges and into the safety glass. I dreamed of Jesus that night, dressed in a fine white suit, sitting in the passenger's seat, bleeding. And, elated, I never ceased to believe that He was the one who'd kept me safe from the sneaky shooter.

It was after a session at the Club one afternoon that I got sick over the death of the Roman soldier, a loss which had occurred years before I'd gotten over my adolescent infatuation with him. I got so upset that I puked on my new bed sheets. Then there was nothing left inside me; I gagged—my bowels clutched and spasmed but all that came out of me was thin yellow liquid. I felt light-headed, losing the feeling of my body.

So many years have passed, carrying their own blessings and curses. I'm known to dwell on the past, not to let things be, to worry about who what why when, so my father often reminds me that everything in life is pre-ordained, that a correct order exists in the events of this world. I want to believe him. I've been driving around Port-au-Prince, looking for some sign that this—the earthquake, the desolation that follows it—is not random. I need a face to hold on to. I want to look an unknown person in the eye, past my own incoherent grief, my own futility.

A man stands next to me. He's in his forties, wearing shorts and an engaging smile. "I'd just come back from Dynamic Club when it happened," he says. "I'd changed into clean clothes and was playing the drums." He turns to point at the house behind us. A pile of rubble. "This is my home," he says. "I had to dig my way out." He sighs. "The house is destroyed, but it's still my home."

A few pedestrians wave at the man. "Moscoso, sak pase?"

A wide, easy grin spreads across his face. "We've lived in Turgeau forever. Everyone knows me in the neighborhood. It's good that they know that I'm still around. Otherwise looters would dig up everything that's been buried." Across the street is the collapsed funeral home Pax Villa, where I attended Junior's viewing.

He is a jolly and playful man, Moscoso, with a laugh as quick as his smile. It seems like he simply erases the bad stuff. There is something about his posture, something dignified, quiet, and settled.

I walk to the end of the street, along the lip where the asphalt falls away into a narrow ditch. I reach Sacré Coeur, where my mother and I kneeled so many Sunday mornings, reciting our Credo. Father André said mass there. From my apartment in Miami, I tried Father André's cell phone after the earthquake. I wanted to speak about religion and God, discuss the meaning of life. I remember he loved beautiful things. Shelves of leather-bound novels, poetry, and art books in his study. Father André had long, strong fingers like those that should play a harp.

He didn't pick up. As the phone burned in my hand, I tried to remember the instant before I learned about the earthquake, the ordinary moment when I leaned against my pillows, watching "Family Guy" in my home in South Florida. Until the phone calls and the TV newscasts about dead bodies and rubble, the moment was indistinguishable from the hundreds of other occasions when I'd turned on the TV and laughed at Stewie, the cartoon.

A large cross remains standing outside the church, which is a kind of beauty. All of a sudden, I fear the Jesus on the cross, as I did as a child. He looks so peaceful, yet threatening. I study the smooth shape of his hands, his face with its beatific expression. I hope to stop believing then, and start cursing God. But the fear goes away.

The roof is still intact, but most of the walls have fallen in. I walk inside the ruins and take in the smell of rotten flesh. The pews are covered with dust. A cell phone and a New Testament have been left behind. Hot afternoon sunlight streams through a crack, and dust particles whirl and jig across the beam, thousands floating up with each new footprint on the dusty floors.

The church is destroyed, but this is still the house of God. Eyes closed, palms pressed together beneath my chin, I mouth a Hail Mary.

When we lived on Christ-Roi Street, not far from Turgeau, my mother and I often visited Sacré Coeur, and every Sunday I hoped to emerge translucent and Catholic, clean as philosophy. The stillness of Christ crucified, candles smoking, Lenten draperies. Rosary clanking. One of the priests often paced the aisles during the sermon. When he stopped, my heart stopped. His eyes searching for sinners everywhere. I tried to be still, unnoticed as a candle before it burns. For many years after that, I positioned myself at a safe distance from God and Satan, tempting both, until I grew closer and closer to God because of that room in the human heart that's older than the body. Sometimes, though, I wish I'd gone the other way so that I could freely cry, "Treason!"

I ache for the peace that faith doesn't bring.

"There's still a body stuck in that small hallway," a voice says. The voice is that of a young man in cut-offs. His hands are thick-veined. He watches me, as he smokes a cigarette. He's got some kind of growth on his neck, shiny and red—a smooth round lump.

He points at a caved-in passage. "The body is right there." His mouth splits into an exaggerated smile, rows of teeth. Then he hides it behind his hand and giggles, head bobbing like a bobbin of thread on a sewing machine. I watch him inhale a slow drag, the sudden surge of orange at the tip, the cigarette firm in his lips.

"Any word about Father André?" I ask.

He shrugs. "Father André is fine. *Just fine.*"

Maybe it's true. Or maybe he doesn't even know who Father André is.

Some people begin to sing outside, huddled in the church garden beneath the sun's hot glare. In another reality, the hymns surrounding me would lift me up. But heat overwhelms me as I stand, still stunned, in the fierce, dry, still air. I go back to the street, walk around a little. Out here, the huge blue sky looms above us, bigger than ever, like it might swallow the rest of us up.

The naked crazy guy who walks by me does not see me. In fact, no one pays attention to me—not the three-legged dog or the old beggar. I watch the slow breath of the dog on its side, stretched out, legs raised a bit so that all three touch the wall, each paw making little shivers. The place where its leg once was is healed over and covered with fur, weirdly beautiful. I wonder if the dog hates the missing leg for leaving.

I hear the flick of a lighter behind me and smell the stream of smoke as the man in cut-offs exhales. I can see into the channel of his ear, a narrow darkness spiraling deep inside his head. He tells me that dogs can feel earthquakes coming. Before the ground shook, the dogs in Port-au-Prince barked and whined, nervous, restless. As he tells me this, the man's eyes jump in the sockets, not completely focused.

"Not everything is lost," the man with the lump says.

He's not looking at me. But maybe he's talking to me. Maybe I will heal, even without understanding or belligerence.

In Poetry Class at the Jail Derek Talks about the Moon

Deborah Cooper

The moon he can see
through the window of his cell

for seven lucky minutes
every night it's clear.

Then Justin talks about the moon
that rose above the barn

on the farm of his seventh
foster family

the way it soothed
his loneliness.

Bart writes a poem about the memory
of moonlight upon snow

when he was only nine,
first time he ran away.

Josh recalls a winter
on the streets, fifteen…

the coldest nights, spent
huddled in a dumpster.

We write in silence then.

When they're led back to their blocks
for lockdown, I head home.

A pale moon sails
the darkening canopy of sky

from wide horizon
to horizon.

V

Where Rain Returns:

Claiming Home

❁

Tattooed

Amy Jo Swing

I'm from mudflats and Matanuska
Milk, duct tape, and blue tarps,
tar melting in earthquake cracks,
sticking to banana bikes and summer shoes.
From first boyloveland and first girl kiss.
From Caribou roaming in downtown
fenced yards, hunted by drunk tourists.
From glaciers shrinking as I grew,
disappearing beyond the view of a Portage
shore. From lands where a man will burn down
his ramshackle house before he'll pay
his damn taxes and another man will steal
a fire engine to save his house from abandoned
wild fires. I'm from Susitna and Chugach, Pioneer
and Denali and all the silt and salmon-laden
rivers their snow flows to. And then into
the sea bays and inlets: Knik, Turnagain,
Katchemak, Seward. I'm from the midnight
sunset and the three o-clock sunset,
where transplanted children sleep with tin foil
over the windows in summer and sun lamps
in the all dark winters. I'm from a place exotic
when away and routine when in it. A square
mile per person, every inch etched in the skin.

Between Time

Mary Kay Rummel

> *"Magnetic fields draw us to Light;*
> *they move our limbs and thoughts."*
> —Rumi

I know this earth—long blades of grass
have probed me, proving full existence—
paint pots of clay, empty silos
ready to receive September wheat,
subdued harmonies of new mown hay,
clouds scarring the heavens with purple.

The sea is not my metaphor
though imprisoned spirits
of the rainbow which once clung
to water and light drift inside me.

These fields of shuck and stack—
their umbratic borders fill me
with spring melt,
with visions, hanging epiphytes, prisms
like stones in the stomach of a swallow.

Rain returns to blown glass air and breath
is a numinous, ripe intrusion.

Directions Home

Kristina Roth

My husband's fraying road atlas is marked with numerous routes home, silver lines carefully indicating all the roads we've covered to and from our destination. My favorite approach is from the west, but the result is the same, no matter which way you come in.

From the south, you'll have covered hundreds of miles of open grassland, usually dry and golden, marked by the meadowlark's song. You'll start to get specific hints of where you're going around Chadron, Nebraska, where a small ridge of ponderosa-covered hills cradles one edge of town. Before long you can see shadows of what lies in the distance toward the west. Indeed, the landscape will flirt with you no matter how direction you approach it.

From the west are several options. You may have crossed the Wasatch Range or the Rockies on your journey; where you're going now isn't quite as grand as those mountains. Coming from the west often involves angling through the southwest corner of the state, where the Wyoming landscape straggles past its borders. Or you can cut up from I-80 crosswise at Rawlins towards Casper, and then approach from I-90. As from the other directions, you will slowly catch clues as to what lies ahead. You're still on the high prairie, gulches with sagebrush appearing here and there. You'll see Devil's Tower on the horizon, and you'll drive over Inyan Kara, the western extent of the Hills.

From the east, on I-90, you cross the Missouri River at Chamberlain and know you're in the West. The green flatness of the eastern croplands changes dramatically here, where a steep drop takes you onto a dam and into West River. Now you're in cattle country, and it's drier and hillier. Collapsing shacks dot the prairie. Ringneck pheasants play chicken with the traffic and often lose. There are fewer towns. At Wall, the spiny silhouette of the Badlands appears. You'll climb the sharp juniper-laced incline after the Cheyenne River. You may get antsy to see the black outlines ahead, restlessly recalling how long this particular stretch always seems. And then you'll drive over a rise and there they'll be: the Black Hills of South Dakota.

Late last April, we had a peaceful drive up. From Houston, we tracked spring's progress through the region by the growth on the cottonwoods and lilacs. By the time we reached Nebraska, the trees were still bare and hawks were easily seen in their branches. Coming out of Chadron, a heavy drizzle covered our path. An hour away from our destination, I could no longer contain my gratitude. "Why are you crying? Is it the rain? Are you afraid?" my husband asked me, a fair guess. "Oh, yeah. You're almost home." The cloud bank blocked the Hills along their eastern side, blocked the faint view of the Cathedral Spires, the Needles, and Mount Rushmore. But I knew they were there.

I don't plan to cry each time as we draw near to home on whatever byway we're following, but my body itself reacts to arriving in the Black Hills: tears, a loosening in my lungs, a feeling of being able to breathe deeper, all of me much more relaxed. These physical reactions begin in small parts along the way. When we lived in California, I'd start to breathe easier once we were well into Nevada or Utah, putting the populations and traffic behind us, moving deeper into the West. From Texas, it usually begins near Amarillo and grows stronger when we move into eastern Colorado. It's all two-lane highway up there, barely anyone on the road. We pass through Lamar, the small cow town where I was born and lived for six weeks. "Can you imagine growing up here?" I ask David every time. My parents decided to return home themselves after my birth.

The Black Hills are scattered with small towns, including Deadwood and Custer, but my sister and I grew up in Rapid City. Even more than the town itself, it is the habitat in which it is situated that has wound its way so tightly around my heart. On each trip, I carry a list of locations in the Hills to visit at least once, if not more. There are those spots near town that are suitable for short trips, such as Falling Rock, the Strato Bowl, or M-Hill. And then there are spots which are deeper into the Hills and require a good half-day, possibly more: Spearfish Canyon, Silver City, or Sylvan Lake. David has come to prefer various spots of his own in the Black Hills and we sometimes must compromise.

A walk along the Flume Trail is always included on my list. The entire trail, once used to carry water for mining operations to the current town of Rockerville, runs about seventeen miles. It's the short section of the trail that follows the edge of Sheridan Lake and then diverts across the lake's dam that I want to see. Just down the gravel road from our little weekend retreat, this trail was like a walk down our neighborhood block when we were kids. It was so familiar and safe that we could take off on our own as though we were heading to the gas station to buy a candy bar. Instead of candy bars, though, we might find large rusty nails from decomposed wooden sluice boxes hidden in the pine needles. The massive slate staircase at the far end of the dam, built by the Civilian Conservation Corps, was a playground to us, whimsical and striking in its old-fashioned design and enormous stones.

Another favorite on my list is the level path behind Silver City and Pactola Lake that follows Rapid Creek for many miles, eventually reaching Deerfield Lake. As a high schooler, I was introduced to this area when I spent much of one summer working on the path with the Youth Conservation Corps. We used axes to hack out new routes or to clear the existing trail of overgrowth, wading and swimming in the creek during our breaks. Marks of previous generations are apparent in this canyon: abandoned concrete bridges from the 1960s, rotting railroad supports poking through the creek's surface, a lilac hedge blossoming in the forest. David and I make slow progress along this path, for one or the other of us is always saying, "Let's stop so I can photograph this." He shoots the tall trees and canyon rims; I try to capture the small details of toadstools, emerging ferns, and wild flowers. We leave the canyon with reluctance.

Less-frequented locations are also on my list: quiet Deerfield Lake, windy Cement Ridge, enchanting Elk Creek Canyon. And there are new places I'd like to see in the empty edges of the Black Hills which push toward Wyoming, or places I've visited a few times but haven't spent enough time at to acquire the same familiarity that I have with other locations. Reviewing a topographical map, I am struck by the many place names that I don't recognize. For all of the hours I have spent in these woods, there is so much unknown. These limits to my knowledge of the area taunt me, make me yearn to explore beyond what I already know.

The man made monoliths that draw many tourists tend to be at the bottom of my list. When you've driven past Mt. Rushmore countless times since earliest memory, there's not much need to stop. The tourist towns of Keystone and Hill City that we enjoyed as pre-teens now seem sadly gaudy, their advertisements for t-shirts and cheap gold jewelry out of place amidst the piney forest. Crazy Horse Monument is impressive, but progress is slow enough that infrequent visits are sufficient. I only go to Deadwood when I visit an old friend. We roam the neighborhoods, where old Victorian houses formerly occupied by the miners from Homestake slowly creep toward the edges of the mountains. This Deadwood is much more interesting to me than that of the shiny lights and bells below.

This spring, we came to the Black Hills northwest through Pine Ridge. I was disoriented by the approach, snippets of the Badlands jumbled together with the foothills, indeed one of the best views of the Black Hills that I've ever seen. The sky was quintessentially western that afternoon, white and gray clouds spread across the blue, casting large shadows on the brown and green prairie below. My mind struggled to place the geography of this approach into the physical framework which I already knew. Unexpectedly, I was seeing home in a new way. Caught unaware, I realized that there may be realities about home that I don't even see yet, in spite of many years of yearning and returning.

This returning home became so remarkably poignant over a decade ago, when I hesitantly understood that I wouldn't be coming back permanently anytime soon. There was college in eastern South Dakota, summer jobs in Chicago and Oregon, work and marriage in Northern California, Central California, and Houston. Every time coming home from these places is an illumination of how much the Black Hills mean to me. The strength of this response was unexpected when it first happened during a trip home from college. Now, the more I see and experience of our country, the more I know where I'd truly like to be.

Every year, I run into strangers who tell me how the Black Hills exerted a draw over them they couldn't ignore, no matter the cost. As I purchase lip gloss for a wedding, the cosmetics associate talks of living in Chicago and earning much more, but coming back when she realized there was nowhere like South Dakota. I meet a shop girl at a junk store who tells me that she's from Pennsylvania and is barely making ends meet here, but she couldn't stay away. At a dollar store, the careworn cashier talks about her struggle with alcoholism and how the Hills are the only thing that have kept her sober. "They're sacred," she says. I couldn't agree more.

On a few of my summer trips back, I'd seen a sedan around town with the license plate *He Sapa*. One quiet afternoon, I visited the new local history museum. Curiously, the *He Sapa* car was in the parking lot. Viewing a short film, I gasped to finally find out what the phrase meant. This is what the Lakota called the Black Hills: *the heart of all that is*. How thrilled I was to have such an accurate moniker for home, even though I know that 'the heart of all that is' is not the same for everybody, even though I am not Native American and find my spiritual truth in Christianity. But for me, it fits. The Black Hills *are* the heart of my world. I'd be a fool to not admit that I've idealized home in some ways; I know my weaknesses and struggles are just the same in South Dakota as anywhere else. But if my very body itself – lungs, shoulders, neck, and more – responds gratefully to being home, there must be some truth in my attachment.

For now, knowing all possible routes home means that I also know all possible routes away from home. I arrive with a list of paths to traverse, but inevitably I must fold up my list until the next visit. Arriving means that I will have to depart again. Sometimes I consider these routes home, the way in which they radiate out of the bull's eye of the Black Hills in crooked spokes. I wonder where my center would be if I had grown up down one of those other routes. I consider that there's more than one way to get there, to get back, and I pray that someday all roads will lead home for me, that my list of paths to walk upon will no longer be limited to occasional visits but will become open-ended and unconstrained.

Blacklock

Vicki Graham

Home ground: we know it
with our bodies, our feet trusting
sand and bog, the slick clay of hard pan.
the spring of spruce duff, the crumble
of sandstone on the cliff's edge.
We know it by taste—thimbleberry,
salmon berry, huckleberry, salal—
and by touch: the stiff curl
of Labrador tea leaves,
the deer fern's brittle spines,
the wiry hair and wrinkled skins of lichen.
Wind and the crash of waves on rock
tell us we are on home ground, and a line
of pelicans gliding up the coast
steadies our hearts, binds us here.

How does a place become home?
What draws the cormorant—
corvus marinus—raven of the sea—
to this rock ledge? What tells
the chickadee, excavate here,
the wrentit, anchor that spider silk
in this forked branch? What leads
the pigeon guillemot to this dark crevice?

Spellbound, we sink into the silence
of the Sitka spruce forest.

Spellbound, we emerge into the wild light
of Blacklock Point where land and water meet
in a crescendo of wave on rock.
Here, on this narrow strip of coast
where pygmy forest, sphagnum bog,
and wind blasted cliffs converge,
we learn that one thrush song
fluting through the trees, one hoarse cry
of the glaucous-winged gull, one flash
of the kinglet's golden crown,
is a single knot in a silken web
that shimmers over the land,
billows over sea stack and ocean.
Here we learn that nothing—seed or egg,
flower or root—is one thing only,
and, if we are lucky, we will see,
just once, the cobalt blue throat pouch
of a male cormorant in breeding season,
the gular skin brilliant as a jewel set in jet.
Here, if we are lucky,
we will know we are on home ground.

Day 212 (When I Am Home)

Amy Nash

I am New England dirt,
the taste of beets out back.
I am not brownstone—
not urban by birth. I am

still in quarry depth,
the scent of cars rusting beneath.
I am not ocher—not red
iron ore impure. I am sipping

fresh water from a claw-foot tub
turned spring, overflowing
to Bone Lake at dusk
and warm. But I am not

the moon to be collected.
I am not forty jokes memorized—
not working a room,
timing accent and plot. I am

ready to mark this laughter
the colors of a flower bed
against brick. I am the line
drawn purple—blues and reds

of a road map
preparing to fold everything
I am
(except magnetic north) in place.

Toward Moorhead, Minnesota

Thom Tammaro

"Held where sky touched land along the edge."
—William Stafford

Dusk. And the last miles toward home.
The dying down of the hard winds
Of the afternoon, the plumes of white
Smoke curling in the evening light,
Tell us we are at the edge of Minnesota.

Returning from the bright cities
Or the places we once called home,
We remember a story told about
Another time, when traders made
This world along other trails:
How in this valley, sleepers,
As if in a dream, were awakened
By the creaks and groans of oxcarts—
Heavy with goods—whose dry oak wheels
Rubbed against ungreased axles, and echoed
Along the miles down the quite valley.

In the rear view mirror we glimpse the dark
Behind us, then look to the road ahead,
To the final windbreak, the sure furrows
and fields reaching for the city's edge,
And then, at last, to the city, itself,
Stretching like a rosary of light, along the river,
The horizon growing wider than our dream.
Traveler, who is listening to the echoes
Of our own history, under the stars of this valley
As we find our way through dusk
And the last miles toward home?

We Live in Texas

Greg Tuleja

We live in Texas now, and Oregon, and Rome,
dispersed, our blind intentions lifted up and cradled down,
toward sleek sea-side apartments, or a dusty border town,
so many, many miles from our home.

It exists now only as the faintest memory,
which should be strong and good, but might not
always be, except for tiny sacred moments,
in speckled shade that quivers on the gate,
a falling breeze, and netted butterflies,
and from the porch, a plaintive cry, come in now,
it's time for dinner, the streetlights are on.

I can see them glowing, and the high hedges,
the basement window, cracked, and the curb
where I used to sit, and I can hear
the milkman clanking, and ice cream bells,
a smell of apples and hot tar steaming in the road,
but as I strain to look inside, I cannot see them,
just the empty room where once they stood.

We live in Texas now, and Oregon, and Rome,
and though we keep a tender heart, we're comforted to learn
that time can never be reversed, and we cannot return
to find our histories, our past, the place we once called home.

Patterns of Home

Sherry Rovig

like a duckling following a dog
I've imprinted on the wrong species
my genius loci for glaciated rolling hills
and farm fields bordered by stands of hardwood, granite boulders
and black raspberries
an aching dream to visit on road trips
eyes hungry for black loamy earth
and green pastures dotted with holsteins
the visceral recognition, somehow always unexpected
like these years in the boreal northwoods
promote a situational amnesia
that dissipates with one corn field

to make a home in a new place
is never easy
walking, always walking
absorbing the shapes of bunchberry and bracken fern
the sounds of drumming grouse and grey jay
the shadows of tall balsam and tang of wild waters

I've imported soil and composted every organic scrap around
hoarding the five inches of topsoil like the finite resource it is
and try to pretend I don't live north of the "tomato line"
cold frames and hoop houses extending the season
finding plants with names like "Siberian tomato" and "Alaskan pea"
careful to check the hardiness zone of each addition

always assuming that my comfort zone is elastic
the "bloom where you're planted" ethos challenged
by late frost and early dark
even while a subtle chemistry is working
and I crave the evergreen air
and company of birch trees

Settled

Marjorie Maddox

It's true, we promised this town and state
we wouldn't bother them, wouldn't dig
ourselves into their coal-veined soil,
into their local rituals and healings.
Burrs in their Pennsylvania wind,
we'd drift, stick at most a year
in these hills four hours from everywhere
flashing, bright, and familiar.

Now, even the weeds call us liars
as we tug their choking gaze
from around our mortgaged home,
comprehend the complexity of roots
suddenly shooting in directions
unpredictable, but as stable
as these rough floorboards
across which we walk nightly
to kiss asleep the children
born surprisingly in this small town
where we wake
each morning to each other.

All of our other lives
are planted deep:
those hacked down,
those waiting to sprout
in some future that will not grow

though watered with fervor.
Still, we look out these streaked windows
and see who we are.

And now, even I,
who hold place as close as Scripture,
am starting to believe.

Buying the Farm, Part B

Karen Donley-Hayes

"I'll be buried next to you, if you want," I said.

Lash had just told me her grandparents weren't sure any longer where Paula, her birth mother, was buried. Paula had died of cancer when Lash was four; Lash still visited her maternal grandparents in Texas on a regular basis.

"We went to visit her grave when I was in Amarillo a couple years ago," Lash said, "and they couldn't find her. They didn't remember where she was anymore." Her mouth twisted; she clamped her eyes down, tears seeping through her dark lashes, newly regrown after that first round of chemo. "I don't want to be alone and forgotten."

How could you argue against that, tell her you would never forget her? She'd seen it happen – her grandparents didn't remember where they'd buried their own daughter. It was irrelevant that they were older, that their memories were failing in general. It made no difference, because it did not change the fact that they *didn't remember* where Paula was. They say there's nothing worse than burying your own child. So, how can you ever forget where the grave is?

Lash, not drifting from her granite position in her marriage, had already mandated that Anton was not to commit himself to a grave next to her. She told me this as we were sitting in her living room, alone except for two Abyssinian cats, the fall sunshine, and Lash's cancer. The cats, a red adult and a blue kitten, scaled the couch and scuttled over Lash, unperturbed by her yellow skin or her bulging liver or her legs that had lost their definition.

"As much as my selfish romantic self in a way wants Anton to pine over me forever," she said, giving a half laugh and swallowing hard, "that really isn't what I want for him. He is such a wonderful person. He'll have a whole life after I die, and he shouldn't obligate himself to being buried next to me. That's not fair to him, or whoever he's with after I die."

"I'll never forget where you are," I said quietly. "I'll be buried next to you, if you want."

By the time Lash and I came searching at Fairview Cemetery in Hiram, all the good spots were taken, long ago occupied. The shaded and sun-speckled lawns, stones overshadowed by gnarled and hoary rhododendrons; the rising hill crowned with mammoth trees and tilting stones so worn by time they stared blind and mute, tired monuments to Civil War combatants lying under them; the subtle and sober slope south of the hill, younger land but still resting in the shade of the hilltop canopy – all this land belonged to others.

We followed the drive out of the tree-and-sun dapples, beyond the foot of the hill, where the lawn slid down a casual grade towards the woods; here, near the edge with a paucity of stones to navigate, the field had been mown by a tractor and Brushhog, leaving stark yellow stalks prickling and stiff. A smattering of lone headstones stood blinking in the afternoon sun; they seemed self-conscious, left out in the elements, as if they wanted to diminish in size, or scooch up the hill into better company. Lash leaned her head against the truck window, looking out over the stubbly grass, then looked back down at the plot map in her hands; she turned it sideways, frowned, tilted her head. When she looked up again, she pointed with the plot map toward the edge of the field.

"There are a few left over there," she said. "And some in the middle here." She tapped the window with the paper.

"You want the middle or the edge?"

She shrugged with one shoulder.

I took a deep breath. "Well, let's see what we got."

We climbed from the truck.

Ahead and to the left, the ground sloped down, steeper. A little footbridge arched over what was probably a stream in wetter weather. Beyond that, trees and brush marched uphill steeply to the backyard of a house.

"What about over there?" I asked.

Lash shook her head. "Too wet." She looked down at the plot map, and continued without looking up again. "I don't want to be pushing up mushrooms any more than I need to." Lash hated mushrooms. "Besides, I don't think it's in the cemetery."

I pelted out a laugh. "Bet the neighbors would like *that*. 'Dammit, they buried dead people on our land again.' " Lash sniggered, her eyes flashing in her gaunt face.

We shifted to drier ground, where the threat of mushrooms was less, and along the eastern edge of the cemetery property, honed in on a stretch of unclaimed plots. Lash reasoned that here, on the property line, no one would crowd our feet when the cemetery eventually filled up.

We settled on three plots along the drive; Lash would be in the middle, and I would be just to her right. The plot to her left might just remain empty forever. ("That way, I won't have to be next to someone I don't know," she'd said, only half joking, not knowing that sometime later, her parents would arrange that some of their ashes would eventually find their way to that third plot.) We looked at the plots, then sat on the ground there. Lash propped against me, and we considered the view we would have, looking east over our feet: disheveled thickets and woods – not the mature hardwoods from atop the hill behind us, where the good grave sites were. This whole section of the cemetery seemed like an afterthought, an addition that didn't mesh with the rest of the place, like an in-law suite tacked on to a century home, concession to supply and demand.

I sometimes wonder what it looked like, what you would have thought if you'd seen us at the cemetery, on that wan early October afternoon – a day in which the chill in the air argued with the tepid sunlight over whether or not summer was over. Would you have seen my unease, my ungainly dance with grief and necessity? Would you have been able to see why we – women not even middle-aged yet – were here, or known I was here at this time only because Lash was *out* of time? Would you have looked at her, standing as she had, hands on hips, appraising the ground, and known how fast she was dying, how soon she knew she'd be buried here?

Sometimes, I think Lash had a list:

Things to do before I die

- Build our house and move to the farm. *Check.*
- Get a horse that's really big enough for me. *Check.*
- Get a blue Abyssinian kitten. *Check.*
- Take the cruise of European capitals with Anton. *Check* (even though it nearly killed her slightly before her time).
- Pick out grave. *Check.*
- I think of the things on that list not checked:
- Be Karen's matron of honor.
- Have a baby.
- Live.

Only a few years ago, we'd purchased our adjoining pieces of farmland. We had planned on spending our lives living on our horse farms right next door to each other. We had planned how we would walk out our doors any time we wanted, and saunter down to our barns, perhaps hack through the woods or down the country roads or to each other's front porches just for the hell of it.

In March, Lash and Anton had moved into the house they had finally built on their land a few years after I'd built my farm on my own land, and for a summer, we lived on our horse farms next to each other.

Now, in October, Lash and I were buying real estate again.

So we sat on the ground, right on top of the graves we'd selected, and leaned against each other. We looked at the diagram of the cemetery, all of the plots marked and numbered, and Lash started to chuckle.

"Look," she said, tapping the map with her pale finger. "Our plots are numbered 61, 62, and 63. Not bad dressage scores." She glanced up at me, that competitive, mischievous sparkle there still, even with her face shrink-wrapping around her skull. "I want the higher score."

We marked our plots on the map, got up off the ground, and left the cemetery.

* * *

Three weeks later, we were back. The cold in the air had overruled the epilogue of summer. Wind blasted sleet under my coat collar. We carried Lash, all 6'1" of her, laid out straight-legged in the plain Amish coffin she had custom-made, to her final real estate.

So now, the crews tucked her into her grave, covered her plain long-enough wood box with dirt, topping it off so that her good-dressage-score-ground was level over her. I blinked at the sleet pellets pinging on the dirt, turning it to slick, frosty mud. *You're not supposed to be here.*

I visited Lash over the winter – sometimes putting the truck in 4-wheel-drive to buck through the snow to our plots – and I visited during the following spring, then the summer, the fall, the winter and spring and summer and fall and winter and every time I visited, I would clamp my jaw and stand on my own grave. I was angry. I'm still angry, I'm not sure at what. Not God. Not Lash. Not me. Not Anton or Lash's parents or the horses or cats or anything tangible. Perhaps I'm angry with inequity. Or impotence. Or the irrelevance of sheer desire to live and force of will.

Anger is tricky when you can't pin it on anything.

Over the years, our stark section of the cemetery has started to fill out a little bit. Slowly, others have planted themselves – bringing with them trees and eclectic shrubberies – so the field looks less like an accessory. In the early spring, sometimes even before the snow has completely forsaken the ground, a smattering of crocuses grows over Lash's grave, popping out of the cold and sodden mud right where friends Laura and Roger had scattered them the spring after we buried Lash. A hydrangea tree, chosen and planted by her parents Bill and Janeen, is doing its slow work at the foot of her grave. Janeen said the tree is their way of being there by Lash now, before they get there permanently. Last fall, wide swaths of its bark disappeared, gone onto some young buck's velvet antlers, and I wondered if the tree would survive the injury. But in the spring, the little tree tossed out leaves and flowers, and the buck rub seemed smaller.

Every time I come here, I still feel a pulse of anger. I stand on my own grave and look at the ground, my face taut; or I prune dead branches off the hydrangea tree, or slip off its dried and finished flowers at the end of the year. Sometimes, I sit on the marble bench that is Lash's headstone – "best friend" is inscribed on it – and just look at our two little plots of land, side-by-side.

Maybe I'll plant a magnolia tree at the foot of my grave to rub shoulders with the hydrangea, to share in buck rubs and sisterhood.

The persistence of ashes

Kenneth Salzmann

In fact, it is the roses that remain.

They enter the house all summer long,
and longer. I place them on the mantle beside the urn
where they will expend their pinks and reds petitioning
what gods they know for the persistence of your ashes.

And they will weep petals across the hearth.

At times, I catch myself believing in the immutability
of ashes, as if we are of this place or any other. As if
the generations that go on spreading like ash will turn
one day to the fixed notion of a place that is home.

The roses were planted fifty years ago or more, a neighbor said,
by a woman who went about, as people do, growing flowers
and growing old, until there was nothing left but roses to testify
that she had ever been. And we set out to make a home amid the thorns
and petals of her life. We nested in the oak-lined rooms that remembered
all her moods and all her movements, but only briefly. And you
took it upon yourself to cleanse and nourish those roses, perhaps in hopes
of sanctifying a transitory life followed seamlessly by ash and bone.

Arriving Home

Jill Hinners

Along this cobble-stoned path
a skin of ice tries to steal my step
as iris leaves, parched
but not yet snowbound,
whisper and rattle in judgment
from their frozen bed.

Some say a ghost lives in this house,
a wife still waiting by the window
for the evening train.
How many years ago
did her husband ride the rails
each day, whistling,
swinging his lunch pail (so light,
so empty, on his return)
until the day of no return,
no whistle save the train's?

Some say the draft
that tonight in the dining room
licks my cheek like a plume
of cold breath is her spirit.
I am a skeptic
but like the story, prefer it
to the diagnosis
"insufficient insulation."

Outside, the irises dance:
undone beauties
condemned to watch the living
carry on living. Inside,
I turn to you without words,
the two of us becalmed
amidst this restlessness of leaves,
a widow's rustling skirts.

75 ½ Bedford Street
The Edna St. Vincent Millay House

Ann McGovern

At midnight, I pace round
the narrow room of the house I love,
only eight and a half feet wide.

I walk hushed, so as not to wake my husband
who would only moan again that the house
is too small and we must move.

He's right. This tiny house does not fit his bulk,
his booming voice, his giant hands.
Yet my candle burns here.

My loom sits in the corner.
In the lamplight, my poems
turn dust to gold. I dig a garden with a silver spoon.

Who will live here next?
Who will grow my strawberries in the patch of earth?
Who will hear my whispering ghosts,

then pick up her pen and write:
"At midnight, I pace round
the narrow room of the house I love,
only eight and a half feet wide."

Two Timing

Sheila Packa

In the old house, a clock.
With each swing of the pendulum, a life span
crossed in less than a minute. A flash of brass

and hidden, a winding key.

I have swung across the floor to music
hand to hand, rough.
Passed a flask, laughed.

Marked the quarter hour, counted night hours
under the moon in an iron bed
slung low to the floor.

Opened the door, closed the glass.

In the crimson heart, a chamber
at arm's reach.
From room to room I fling the dark

myself in it.
Beginning, ending,
too far, not far enough.

Any evening in early December

Marge Piercy

Orange flames tipped blue and green
waver in the fireplace, make dance
patterns on our eyelids.

The kitten sprawls carelessly
showing her spotted belly. The Brown
Brothers form and circle of fur.

Bach's 4th cello partita is playing.
Occasionally a log snaps sharp
as a flamenco dancer's feet.

You are sipping bourbon. I
eat a chocolate truffle. The fire
sighs like an old gouty man

and goes to ashy sleep.
We trade yawns. Very soon
we'll retire to bed followed

by a posse of cats. They'll
wait politely till we are finally
still, then pile on top.

How hard and long I traveled
to reach this quiet place.
How lucky I feel.

Nesting

Gary Boelhower

With all the green threads of hope
in the fine weave of your body,
make me a nest in the branches
of your arms. Make it warm
against the storm. Gather the tender
grasses softened by the weight
of sorrow and snow, the abandoned
kite string woven in the fingers of oak,
pieces of purple yarn from the mitten
still clenched tight in the fist of ice,
and dreams, plenty of spring dreams.
Stitch it all together with your closest
attention, interlace the laughter
and the pain, braid the strands
of gladness, grief, longing.
Line the safe circle with the softest
down stolen from the warmth
close to your heart. Then, call me
with your song. Do that dance
with your fancy feathers. Lure me home.

Looking Out My Bedroom Window

Jane Yolen

Once a field where day and night
rabbits, possums, turkeys, deer,
even bobcats and bears crossed the long grass,
predator and prey, you know—
that old exciting story full of danger.
Now my daughter's cozy Cape,
the slatey blue of a February sky,
lets me know with window light
that she and my granddaughters
are safe, eating, showering, reading,
the homey stuff, not fight and flight.
The bobcat still crosses, unafraid,
through her back garden some days.
The bear occasionally strides down her driveway,
glancing hungrily at the kitchen door,
exclamation point reminders of times passed.
We give away wild for comfort,
for safety, for family, forever,
but sometimes it is a story,
the story we need to hear.

A Gay Doll House

Kenneth Pobo

I put four thin chops in the oven,
boil water for corn. Am I
mimicking my mother's routine,
you my dad just home from the lab,

she getting dinner ready by 5:30?
Do you mimic your dad when you
mow the lawn, fix my computer,
fire up the Weber grill? Or are we

imitating no one,
ourselves at last,
conversations painting the rooms
colors our folks would never choose.

Now It's a House

Lowell Jaeger

Now it's a house all my own, I say,
as I watch your tail lights fade
and the kids in the backseat wave
goodbye. I stare down the empty
drive, try to remind myself I should be glad.
Then clear the breakfast leftovers,
still warm, your napkin secretly unfolding
itself as I carry your plate
across the kitchen. Till I spy
the lipstick kiss in the creases

and I'm tempted by the scent
of you to write all this down,
the nameless art of lives entwining.
No simple task, and the cause
I've little else accomplished late
in the afternoon ... but this promise
to tell you how these same walls and floors
are not the same when you're not in the room.

How this house when it's all my own
is lusterless as I am without you.
How I roam kitchen to dining room, upstairs and downstairs,
while the furniture fidgets in the uncomfortable silence
of one man's mumblings. Or I muse
over something you said, the language
that passes between us unspoken. Maybe
I stop, press to my face the sleeve of your coat
where it hangs on its peg in the hallway. Or laugh at myself

peeling potatoes at the sink, the sunset burning
orange across the lake outside the window, the thought
of you standing soon here beside me kindling
a glow on my horizon. I light candles. Turn the stereo
low and soothing, our favorite Spanish tunes.
Your plate, fork, knife, spoon, and the kids' and mine
each in place. Your headlights flash up the drive.
Smell the roast bubbling in its juices?
Same wall, floors. Everything's the same
and not, I say.

Now it's a home.

My Place

Joseph A. Soldati

Here is there when I'm away.
I miss my clowns—cats
Roxanne and Tramp, even
the little rocks from the litter box
they leave on the rugs.
I miss my study—the epic hubbub
of writers and writing, books and papers
illumined by the Macintosh.
(Shakespeare wishes he had had one—
What light from yonder Windows breaks?
Wordsworth and Thoreau glad they had not.)

When I'm not here,
the walls might as well be bare—
no "Freight-yard at Pullman,"
no "Moon Walker," "Mykonos Matron,"
or "Caribou on the Horizon."
I miss my kitchen—my fingers
smelling of garlic, great pots
steaming, my mouth tasting the sauce,
the expectations of friends at table,
hilarity amid the empty wine bottles.
I miss the deck above the river—
the grain ships going to India—
and, at night, streetcars like necklaces
adorning the black bridge,
the moon rising over the city.
I miss the big bed—
my Elysian Field where you
may finally find me.

The Permeable World

Rachel Barenblat

All the world is a room made of windows
with different views through every pane

sit with me, knock two bowls together
hold an *etrog* carefully in both hands

watch me gather palm and myrtle and willow
and turn in every direction, hoping for gifts

from the winds that quake the aspen,
from the earth, from the spiraling fire

last Sukkot you were snug inside, but
now you've joined the permeable world

when the rains come the roof leaks
but you're safe in my arms

and at night we're surrounded by angels
twinkling on all sides, escorting us through.

Five Summer Nights

Susan Elbe

One   a night before you know what's happening

No talk, just radios, tube-lit
and murmuring: on the back porch,

White Sox double-header night games:
in the kitchen, Inner Sanctum:

in the bedroom, rhythm & blues,
static sparking in your fingers:

a streetlight's precision cutting
tool slices dark into slivers:

the dirty-sock sky of August
low-down and wet: a train whistle,

faint smell of coal and burnt thistle:
tea roses unfurled by the fence,

lipstick-pink, neon as milk-teeth
and fever: the doors coming loose.

Two   a night when you do

In this house, we're all zippers and
buttons, opening and closing

with the weather: we're yeast and salt
and sometimes milk or burnt toast:

rank coats huddle in the closet,
the bathtub has claws, and each clock,

a different time, each face, its own:
the tap water's sweet and we do

our best, but it's not good enough:
we know nothing about magic,

though at dusk everything takes on
a loose blue, the edges fall off,
corners disappear: in that light
our wings can take us anywhere.

Three anthropomorphic

You're the town I want to live in,
the one that has no lake, but

where the furry air is salted
as tomatoes and packing heat:

days unchangeable except when
weather rolls the waves of switch grass:

true, I'll leave you, go back to the city
but until I do: show me how

to shoot this tin-can loneliness
off fence posts, claim this place as mine:

Lord, let me come as a stranger
with a wet stone under my tongue:

tether my feet to dust, the boat
I've been building, smithereened.

Four a night from the inside

Branches scrape at the screen: a bad
wind breaks in, stinking of river,

scrieving paint-peeled sills, twisting in
the curtain-folds: damp paper dolls,

stuck to linoleum, flap thin
arms: in the cellar, dusty jars

of tomatoes sing: electric
fences spit blue and cows bellow,

wild-eyed, knee-deep: in drowned fields
dead mice float and the cistern fills:

in fractured moonlight, flimsy skirts
of tiger lilies drag in mud:

the floors tilt toward drop-off: years
away, we hear the bridge let go.

Five the hardest night

Solstice. And the stubborn daylight
goes on and on until finally

you can cup the apricot moon
in your hand, drink in its distance:

you take the only, thirsty road,
carry water far, fall asleep

bone-tired, your attention aching,
stretching out: all night, by seed-light

you search in dream, knowing nothing
tells you how far from here to there,

from one love to the next: Drifter,
your heavy pollen-dusted wings

the sweet cello of your body—
too freighted to go deep enough.

Mending the Net

Based on the painting by Thomas Eakins, 1881

Martin Willitts, Jr.

We gather as a community, prepared to mend.
Forgiveness is in the air.
If we do not restore trust, it will haunt us as a storm moving in.
The fabric of love demands patching.
We begin our solemn task, bent to this renovation.

We gather at *The Meeting Tree*—a place where we go to
after a storm to make sure all is accounted for.
Anyone missing is an untangling of the net.
Let no one be lost. Anyone misplaced shall be found—
Let not one body will be mislaid.

We will spread our net far and wide.
We congregate at this wisp of a tree where our answers
are prayers. We inspect what we have made
and find it maddeningly wanting. There are gaps, rends,

some small as a gull's eye, some are bigger than grief.
Nothing cannot be repaired without hard work.
Listening to suggestions is fishing of a religion.
Without a community, there is no sharing.

If we lack that, we swim as minnows within the silence.
We are making what was broken into whole.
Fishing has taught us patience.
We throw away what we do not need.

When someone is missing, we diminish into the amount of loss.
We pursue a horizon as it stays far ahead,
uncertain as to when to haul in our cast nets.
We rely on instinct to stop and repair what needs it.

It is like knowing when to pray
and when it will not suffice. We are entangled
in the sharing, as words swim by too small for catching.
We are never done with mending promises into the sky.

We catch conversation in nets of assurances.
When we are done, we return to the way things were before.
We do not look back, for there is work ahead.
The light is fully upon us, as we take back every bad thing we said.

Patriotism

Ellie Schoenfeld

My country is this dirt
that gathers under my fingernails
when I am in the garden.
The quiet bacteria and fungi,
all the little insects and bugs
are my compatriots. They are
idealistic, always working together
for the common good.
I kneel on the earth
and pledge my allegiance
to all the dirt of the world,
to all of that soil which grows
flowers and food
for the just and unjust alike.
The soil does not care
what we think about or who we love.
It knows our true substance,
of what we are really made.
I stand my ground on this ground,
this ground which will
ultimately
recruit us all
to its side.

VI

The Contours of Private Geography:
Musings on the Meaning of Home

Always Home

J. P. White

At home, broken home, a home away from home.
Seems clear enough that the sourcebook
of our affections can also feed our deepest wound,
the entries regarding our origin written in tears
commingled and scarcely remembered.
When my Cincinnati grandfather died young,
and the preacher said he was called home,
I knew then I wanted always to live home free,
traveling by the light of happenstance.

How wrong could I be, in my blend of happen
and circumstance, if Jesus backed me up
when he said foxes have holes, birds have nests,
but man has nowhere to lay his head? Lost
might just as easily be found which is how
I like it. A little bit lost. A little bit found.
Like now, sitting here, by the sailboat harbor
watching the mauve light angle in the willows,
hoping some skipper will arrive, another will leave.

Home

Gloria Frym

During the waning years of the 20th century and well into the next, one could commonly witness homeless, unsheltered souls perform the most intimate actions under the glare of public light and community revulsion. A man in an alley holds up a piece of mirror, shaves, pats Aqua Velva on his cheeks; another man finishes defecating in the shadow of a vehicle; a toothless couple leans against a mural, a picnic of burrito innards spread before them on salsa stained pages of the *San Francisco Guardian*. (A young man stops to take their photograph with a Hasselblad. How to view this?)

Home is form, the order nature requires of its earthly constituents. And humans, the most flexible and easily transplanted of the creatures, make home with or without root or ownership. Home is a private refuge. Then there are the Wandering Ones. Exile has been their historical fate, a people forced to reinvent or replicate home everywhere on earth, and cling, when threatened, to a spiritual homeland. They may not recall their origins, but live their losses in hostile, constant reconfiguration of form, which contains all the ancient mysteries of tribes who once thrived side by side.

Home is both interior as emotion and exterior as materiality. Home is the source of memory and memory's companion, imagination. *I always ran Home to Awe*, Dickinson writes more than once. All our senses are coded in ideas of home. Home is both parental and dependent. It nurtures by providing a site of creation and procreation, a cradle, a resting place, and it demands care and feeding in return. *Occupation: At Home* reads Dickinson's obituary. And her tombstone reads *Called Back*.

There is the symbolic power of home. Consider the descendents of Jews, and Moors, banished from Spain, who have passed down through the violent centuries the original keys to homes occupied by their ancestors—skeletons of place and origin—now nearly a dream but always actual, no matter the distance in time. The room, the door, the lock gone to other forms—but the key still in the sunlight.

Seeking Sanctuary

Wendy Brown-Báez

A few years ago a friend called me from Jerusalem. I was relieved to hear his voice. He had previously written to tell me that when he came home from work, he could hear gun shots in the street. His apartment was close to a Palestinian neighborhood from which rockets were being thrown. Now helicopters circulated overhead. We chatted for a while about the current crisis.

"The moderates have become more right-wing," Moshe told me.

"I know the young people on both sides, in the army and in the camps, grew up during the Intifada and were taught to hate," I replied.

"The patience of Israelis with Arafat and Israeli politicians has disappeared," he said. "Here is a hypothetical situation," Moshe continued. "If the American Indians had an uprising and demanded all the land back, what would you do?"

I laughed. "I'm the wrong person to ask. I would give it back. Although, of course, that is unrealistic. And a very different situation. Since the Native Americans revere the land spiritually and ecologically, it might be in better hands."

While spending a month in Oaxaca, I brought along Neruda's book of poems called *Isla Negra.* In the foreword, Alastair Reid says that it was not a systematic autobiography in poem form "but a set of assembled meditations on the presence of the past in the present." It followed the chronology of his life. "This is cool!" I thought. "I could do that. I could write poems about the places where I have lived." I made up a 1ist, starting with the first sub-let when I moved out of my parent's home in Pennsylvania after high school. I was stunned to count forty-two places, not including the *casita* I was currently renting in Oaxaca. The locations started on the East Coast, went to the Southwest, zigzagged all over the West, from Colorado to Seattle, from Montana to California. My travels culminated in an exodus out of the country to Belize and Mexico, over to Spain, the Canary Islands, Greece, and Israel.

No wonder I related to the Jewish people! When I arrived off the boat in Haifa, I felt as though I had finally come home, returning from exile to sanctuary. Traveling throughout the states and across the ocean was with a group of people and never felt like homelessness because we lived the same lifestyle. We owned one set of clothes, following our mantra, "Travel light." We lived a life of self-discipline, ignoring personal comfort, having few material possessions.

But did I live this nomadic lifestyle simply as an imposition of the dictates of our "guru" or was it the natural result of my yearning to travel as a child? I daydreamed of hitch-hiking to exotic places, of being a Gypsy and a wanderer. I had an insatiable curiosity about the world and the people in it, a desire to be "footloose and fancy-free." When I stuck my thumb out on the side of the road, slept on Spanish beaches, or hiked up curving forested roads, I was not aware that here was my day dream come to life. I never thought to myself, "Gee, this is exactly what I asked for when I was young."

At the time, it seemed natural as rainwater and as commonplace as the Dodge grinding to a halt to pick us up.

The commune dissolved during the time we were in Israel, leaving me to cope with re-identifying myself, renting my own apartment and raising two boys as a single mom. Although I no longer lived with the group, I still ended up moving. After I returned to the states I counted six moves until I settled in the condo I shared with my life partner Michael, where I lived in the same building a whole twelve years! I was so tired of moving at this point, that if the condo burned down I thought I might camp in the ashes. I couldn't fathom packing another box, giving away more stuff, sifting through the mementos, books, and collections I never used to have and which now overflowed our home.

I was happy to return after every trip where my place was held for me like a marker in a book. I received mail. I actually bought address stickers. The wanderlust had gone out of me.

It took me a long time to recuperate from leaving Israel. It was the first time I ever felt homesick. I understood finally the attachment to a particular land. I missed the Mediterranean Sea, the golden light that seemed to surround each person, the dynamic passion, innocence and naiveté mingled with practical commonsense. I missed the taste of Goldstar beer, ripe tomatoes, juicy oranges and warm bread or piping hot pita and the varieties of olives. I missed the color and smells of the *shuk*, the rhythm of the holy days, the joy people took in children and their passion for politics, intellectual dialogue and history. I missed the melodies of the Hebrew language. Most of all, I missed feeling inspired, on fire, impassioned myself. I was terribly in love with the land, with the people, with the scorching fire of truth that I encountered there.

The Oregon coast was breath-taking. The crisp mountain air of Colorado was invigorating. The warm laziness of California was peaceful. The heart-felt warmth of the humble Mexicans was comforting. The dignity of the Spaniards was intriguing. But never had I fallen in love before.

Ultimately Israel could not remain a permanent sanctuary for me. The land and her people embraced me while my life shattered and was re-configured in ways I had never thought possible. The breakup of the commune forced me to confront who I was and what I truly believed. I had to provide a home for my children. Although I had arrived on a tourist visa, I got a job as a nanny and my employers included us as part of their family. Eventually more children joined us, a multicultural mix of Jews, Arabs, and Americans. The elderly neighbor downstairs made sure I had propane, watched the soccer match on tv, and didn't eat *hametz* (anything with leavening) over Passover. My friends took me out to dance at the disco and sat around my table until the wee hours of the morning, discussing who knows what in Hebrew. But Israel's own unsteady political situation began to totter under the dual pressures of the Intifada and the Gulf war. When the mothers I worked for gave me instructions to take their toddlers into the sealed room during an air raid and the neighbor came up to ask me if we had picked up our gas masks yet, I felt I must leave. Back in Pennsylvania I fretted and worried, my eyes glued to CNN. With anguish in my heart, I prayed for those I had left behind.

Once I put a map of the world in my son's room and we marked with push pins all the places where we had lived. When he bought a house, I reminded him that he was very young to have such responsibilities. A house ties you down, I told him. He had planned a vacation to come see us in Santa Fe but had to wait because the refrigerator needed repairs and it was time to re-paint the outside of the house.

"I know, Mom," he replied. "But all I ever wanted is my own house." I guess that is to be expected after all that moving around which I had hoped would enrich him. But he craves the settled security of my parents' lifestyle, the one I was desperate to break away from, the one I was anxious to leave behind as I explored alternatives. Even as I appreciated each place that held me and my things, I knew I could leave it all in a flash—pack up my photo albums and my CDs. I know it is possible to live with almost nothing, to sleep on a beach or on a train station bench, to wash in a stream, to eat from a left-over picnic.

Moving to Minnesota was the last thing I ever thought I would do. My son asked if I could come and help with childcare. I knew I wanted to be a part of their lives, wasn't I already complaining about the distance between us? After Michael's death, the condo was legally inherited by his mother and I had to leave behind everything once again, despite my resistance. The hand- picked ceramic tiles that had replaced the worn kitchen linoleum. The red door I had painted to bring in positive energy. The rocking chair, my gift to Michael on our anniversary, and the armoire he had given me for Christmas. The view of the mountains and the petunias I planted every spring. It took me weeks to sort through all of my things and decide which to keep in storage and which I could ship or carry in my suitcase. It took another two years to ship the rest.

But we know that things do not make a home, although being surrounded by my treasures makes me feel more at home. And an enticing culture or a favorite spot do not make a home, although they contribute to the sense of ease and comfort, a sense of belonging. Even friends do not make a home, although they bring joy to one's home. A home is something carried within one's own heart that can be unfolded to include whoever you are with, wherever you are. With a scarf draped over a table, I can create an altar, set a photo and a bowl into which I place rocks or seashells, glass hearts or Milagros, dried flowers or coins. With a small jewelry box, I can bring my favorite earrings and remember that the last time I wore them we were dancing on my birthday. With photographs, I can reminisce about my son's first football game, the last beach walk before I flew back to the states, or the bougainvillea in Mexico. With a poem, I can put those memories on paper to keep forever.

What makes a home is the feeling of sanctuary. It is a place of respite from the world or an invitation for someone to join you, a place of intimacy with yourself and loved ones, a place that is designed to be a reflection of who you are, what you love, where you've been, and your hopes and dreams. Looking back, I realize that I carried all of that with me wherever I landed, in simple gestures, by my own personal style. The way I draped a *rebozo* over a chair, placed books on a shelf, arranged flowers in a vase or a picture on a wall.

But the Gypsy is still there, listening, waiting for the call, the call to move on, to taste and explore, to risk oneself. The Gypsy knows that we are human beings sharing this one planet and that everyone needs love, attention, and respect. The Gypsy would give back the land to the Indians and inter-marry with the Palestinians, desiring peace more than national boundaries, and faith more than religious contempt. Even though I belong nowhere, I belong everywhere. I am an earthling. And that gives me a sense of security that no government, no army, no borders, no allegiance to a belief can ever give me.

Be-long-ing

Farzana Marie

noun.

1. A personal item that one owns; a possession. Often used in the plural.

2. Acceptance as a natural member or part: a sense of belonging.

My first friend in the Arizona desert
was an Iraqi refugee.
After a father's death,
after high-tailing it under veil of dark,
after years in a Syrian camp
she was here:
a desert with a different tongue.

In her language *bayt* is house
and *bayt* is also a line of poetry.

Poems as dwellings.
That seemed right,
so that when one made of mud,
beams or marble
toppled, burned, was overrun,
you'd still have the one
made of curved words,
the one you could slide into
just in time:
safe.

One year our nomadic clan met
in a borrowed house,
where from Mom's bulging suitcase
Christmas materialized:
stockings deftly shuffled into position,
extemporized decorations marched
to adorn a startled potted cactus;
tangle of fingers fashioned dough
into coconut-sprinkled stars,
then in long-standing tradition
addressed birthday cards to him
whose delivery far from the sharp halls
of modern hospitals
formed a crevice in history.

There it was. Home.

Story like a fire-lit cabin to a lost,
frost-bitten hiker in the high country.

The place your soul breathes out,
realizing it was holding its breath.

Photo taped to inner skin
of dust-encased Kevlar helmet.

Maybe not a door we'd walked through
but a place we all recognized.
Not a song we could name
but notes we could all hum—
a colored light slipping in
through pain-tinted windows,
a dampness on the shoulder,
an ancient, knowing whisper.

Rituals of December

Joyce Lombard

I sit with friends,
remember what parents brought
to our childhood homes
in this bleak month,
remember light, colors, small villages,
wreaths with electric candles
brightening winter windows
as bombs fired up skies
over Germany and France,
remember how mirrored lakes appeared
in unused fireplaces
though England was cold and hopeless.

Somewhere in adult hearts
home meant magic
where children could be held
safe. This year
I place wreaths,
light candles
in my blessed world,
hold in my heart the women of Syria,
Israel, Afghanistan,
support their hope
of homes in which to light candles.

In Common

Naomi Shihab Nye

I'd been a little worried about our luncheon.

Two lovely retired women who had never met before would be eating Vietnamese noodles together on a hundred degree day—and they could not be more different. I'd invited them both without really considering it.

One was a beloved college professor of English, now living in a quiet gated community with her 104-year-old second husband, a great intellectual. I had studied Gertrude Stein with her in college. We had always stayed in touch.

The other, who most likely had never heard of Gertrude Stein, was recent owner of a resale shop in a Victorian mansion on the edge of downtown. For decades, she had carefully arranged delicate laces, embroidered tablecloths, vintage glassware and overstuffed chairs for her customers. You could take her the silver tray you got for your wedding and never used, or your auntie's hand-embroidered footstool, and she would sell it for you, writing out old-fashioned receipts on a tablet with carbon papers. I bought ancient postcards there. Random plates. She only kept 10% of any sale price. On the day her husband died in his sleep, she told me she put on her make-up before calling 911. "I knew it was going to be a long day." Frank, funny, she still answered the telephone as if she were running a business—"Good afternoon, this is Mrs. S…"

But the two women didn't seem like people who would have much in common. One was elegant and highly educated and the other, a talkaholic with thirty unsold lamps stuffed in her attic.

Somehow, by the time we were polishing off the last of our tasty noodle bowls and tall glasses of iced water, my professor friend mentioned growing up outside Fort Worth.

Mrs. S. perked up. "So did I."

The professor said, "I grew up in Bowie." Mrs. S. said, "Nocona!" Their towns had been forty miles apart in Montague County, Texas.

Mrs. S. mused. "I remember Bowie. When I was three, I was taken there, to the county hospital. My brothers and I cried in the car. Our father, who worked in the oilfield, had been injured by a piece of malfunctioning equipment that plucked his whole stomach out—he could not be saved. One-by-one we were taken into his hospital room to say goodbye. He told me to take care of my brothers. Oh my. The Bowie Hospital. It seems amazing he was even able to talk after what had happened to him. But he said goodbye to each one of us. It was the day everything changed for our family."

The professor was staring at her hard. "Well," she said, "when I was five, I was taken into a room in that very same Bowie Hospital and my sick mother said to me, "If I die, you will have to go live with Aunt Frieda and Uncle Maynard." I was stunned. She died shortly thereafter. It was the last time I ever saw her. Everything changed for me in that hospital too."

I had never heard of the hospital or even Montague County, though I have lived in Texas forty years. The same small-town building, hundreds of miles from where we sat in downtown San Antonio, had been the scene of heartbreak for both my dear friends' childhoods. They had never before mentioned their young parents' deaths to me, either.

They locked hands on the table and stared at one another. They shook their heads, said, "I declare," "That's just unbelievable," "Oh my, the Bowie Hospital."

*

I can't help thinking—what if all the people who oppose one another could pause at meal tables together before any killing or disaster occurs and say—*So where did you live? What happened to you? What was the worst thing? What have you seen?*

If they talked long enough, would there always be something that linked them? Like that degrees-of-separation thing, but more a degrees-of-similarity or synchronicity? Would there always be a way to make a bigger home together? A way to belong to the same world, instead of different, allegedly conflicting ones?

An American and an Afghani, say? A liberal Pakistani and a conservative Pakistani? Syrians and Iraqis and Republicans and Democrats, a Palestinian hanging on to his home and a Jewish settler from Brooklyn trying to seize it—would there still be something?

Maybe to do with food or a dream or a terrible unresolved sorrow? Maybe a tree or a cow or a mountain or a baby or a field?

We walked out of that restaurant in a bit of a daze. Strange, but now, tears in my own eyes, it was hard to say goodbye to the two brave Montague County girls who survived it all, such rough farewells and early loneliness, so long before today's bright sun ever baked the cars on the street.

Fault Lines

Cynthia M. Baer

From the ridge
earth folds back on itself,
hills curve up and over and down
along a line of fault and fear

solid earth
threatens solidity,
riddles expectation: the ground
we stand
        slips,
        slides
                        plates inch
toward cataclysm;

soils we think firm, forever true,
ride swells of fluid rock rising
and falling like the sea
with the pull of the moon

primal ground, palingenesis
of our daily geography.

*

At the ridge
earth and sky meet divide: fall
into origin—light and dark, high and
low, father, mother—always together

forever apart; balanced in
their distance and the tiptoe dance
of daily departures

and returns,

dinners made

and missed

their fault lines, our bedrock.

In such faulted ground
the I travels a line
of infinite resistance, fear
forever foregrounding collapse
youth learns to take her balance; I
the solitudes of self-contained pleasures
books and sun, adolescent sex—
the mimed gestures
of a close-curved elegance;
you two, each your own heady version
of seventies turbulence: beads,
fringe, smoke and song—
the sudden death of drugs

separate paths, yet each somehow
got on, learned to step uncertain
ground, dance the rim of darkness
in daily fear counterpoised, bound
to that common center, home.

*

Home. That ground whose depths we
cannot plumb, whose paths we daily trace, yields
the contours of private geography—
homes, husbands, a child for me, for all
careers. Fortysomethings now, we
stumble along lines of least resistance
          divorce,
                    petty dissent,
                              private disrepair
the ground beneath our feet,
familiar, uncertain, we stand
each precarious in
solitary circle,
seeking ground, avoiding return:
home's not where the heart is.

It is where strength is.
Along the fault earth rises full
folds back into herself,
darkness unknowable,
shadowed in light that slants
from a limitless sky;
between, we stand our ground:
three who have long balanced
the ridge of fault and fear,
resistant to our fall,
may learn yet to revel
in a darkness we make light
and float upon the solid rock.

Along Highway 1

Keiko Lane

"So many yellow flowers: suns each one."
—*Mimi Khalvati*

I'm crossing a coastal creek with a friend the morning after her late night email declaring *bring boots and clothes that can get muddy. I have an adventure in mind.* We drove forty minutes in her car, stopping at a mid-day, mid-week farmer's market for salads and crackers that tingled our tongues with sharp fennel. I follow her booted steps across a mossy shaded creek and lean deeply into the rough, moss-carpeted bark of a tree at its bank, until finally trees open into a field of suns, the bright sun overhead casting its own gold onto the ocean below.

Driving the misty coastal road to her house that morning I heard a report on the radio: since 1995 the number of preschool age toddlers on antidepressants and Ritalin has tripled. Doctors and researchers on the radio discuss the phenomena, saying *well yes of course the drugs aren't tested on children that young, so we don't really know how they affect the long term development of neurotransmitters, but these parents are overworked and tired and we watch the children acting out of control during our short visits with them while we take their histories from their parents...* I imagined my cousins' children watching their frantic cartoons, keeping up with the explosions of Power Rangers and clutching the hard, slick plastic of a Gameboy in their chubby hands.

My own hands tightened on the curve of the steering wheel as the road turned towards tall eucalyptus staining the air with their sharp, blue-sage smell. Local farmers want to uproot them because they are not native to this place, and so they overwhelm the more fragile, local plants.

Some reports say that eucalyptus was first introduced into California during the gold rush. Shortages of timber made the sturdy, fast growing tree appealing for building, fuel and trade. My parents' house is set into a deeply sloped Southern California hillside. Over the years my parents dug and cut terraces into the hill, some for decks, some for trees which lean heavily with citrus all year, and the bottom terraces for gardens my mother planted when I was small because she wanted me to know how things grow. We planted corn, tomatoes, beans. When I got tired of helping her I would run circles around the large eucalyptus tree separating the garden from the redwood swing-set my father built. I know it isn't this simple. What plants didn't grow in our yard because of the intense, deep roots and constant shedding of those hundred year old eucalyptus? What birds do I not recognize because they couldn't nest in those trees?

My uncles, my mother's brothers, were Southern California strawberry farmers until they retired. One uncle still keeps a large plot of land, passed down from my grandmother, with long, clean rows enough to keep the entire extended family in shallots, garlic, onions, tomatoes and squash all winter. And for most of the year, strawberries. As a small child I used to look down the rows of strawberries on the farm, and not know how to focus my eyes with no trees to gauge the distance between me and the very far away end of the row.

What does it mean to be native to this place? A poet I know, an Esselen woman, was told by a white anthropologist that her tribe, native to the California coast, had died out. The story told to her in passive construction, as though they had not been slaughtered in the missions. As though she were not standing there to hear the story.

On the way to meet my friend I drive past an apple tree, hard red fallen fruit untouched under the craggy base. Lone tree far from an orchard. Apple orchard. *Manzanar.* Internment Camp. Where my mother was born. Where my uncles, so far removed from their homeland stood at the barbed wire fence on sunny days, watching cars pass on the highway, and ran races the length of the fence. So different from the childhood afternoons I spent walking the perimeter of the sloped yard, running my fingers over the soft yellow tips of wild mustard and sour grass whose stems I would suck, a shiver down my spine at the tingle and pucker at the back of my throat from the sour juice. Flowers the same yellow as the round button that sits on my dresser. It reads *Yellow Power,* with the delicate black line drawing of a hand holding *hashi,* chopsticks, between relaxed fingers. My mother doesn't remember where she got the button, nor do I remember when she gave it to me, or, more likely, when I took it one childhood afternoon of sorting through the rarely touched jewelry box next to her bed.

I turned back to the radio to hear the next, isolated report about the California proposition, expected to pass, that will put fourteen year olds in adult jails. I imagined children as young as my cousins' babies carrying the bright colors of their Pokemon cards, the children I knew years ago, refugees to Los Angeles who had lost their homes, escaping from the wars in El Salvador and Nicaragua, faces upturned toward any trace of warmth in a crowded prison yard. Last week a therapist at San Quentin asked his group of inmates what it would be like to have children in the jail. He said that room went silent for a long moment of inhaled trembling, until one man said *you don't want to know,* and the therapist said *yes, I do,* and again the man said *no, you don't* into the silence of the room.

Last night on TV a young boy in a class where a policeman was telling them how to avoid being hurt by a stranger asked the officer *what if the person hurting you is your dad?* Driving north along the ocean this morning to the friend whose father hurt her, I opened the window to the cry of a hawk overhead circling above the eucalyptus, wind pushing against the fine hair on my arms until it felt like the nerves were exposed and raw, and my chest ached with want and fear, though I could not name a source. I took one hand from the wheel and turned off the radio. I listened to the tape of a poet friend reading about the cold coastal drive in a state we'd once shared, her voice exhaling...*until the fog begins to lift over the bay...* until I noticed the break open into sun ahead of me as the fog began to rise in great sheets over this bay into a thousand suns reflecting on the water.

On the other side of the coastal creek, we search for some dry ground in the field of wet daffodils, their petals soft against our skin, the stalks cracking under our feet though we try to walk around them. From the middle of the field we stand quiet together, arms filled with flowers, watching the sun on the water until the fog begins to settle along this coast we have adopted as our own. We rise from one fog into another.

Threshold: Four Steps Toward Home

George Roberts

Starting Place

As you cross the field on a snowy day, a syllable of wind can alter your path, push a corner of your collar up to your cheek, hold it there against gravity. In a distant city, a phrase of steam drifts from an abandoned warehouse. And when you find your footing again, your collar dropping back into place, that lost moment, that instant when your life went on without you. Sometimes fairy tales can save us when we are lost. You remember standing, before there were seatbelts, by your dad's shoulder as he drove the blue station wagon, listening to him tell of *Hansel and Gretel* or *The Golden Ball.* You were five and the darkness a long way off. Later, on the drive home, you pushed the back seat flat and lay down, watching through the darkened window the stars, your as yet unborn brothers and sisters, whirling across the night sky.

The Meaning of Home

All winter crows assemble in the barren trees, calling to each other at dusk, distracted parents summoning their children in from play. Sometimes far enough away that you faintly hear them. Other times just above you when you go outside, sooty smudges like hints of leaves, speaking to you, personally. Crows are smarter than we give them credit for. They know who you are, that you are not a threat. They know things about your heart you are not aware of, the cold weather of your father's furrowed brow. If, instead of greeting them with a glance upward and a nod, you threw a stone, word would spread. The brittle glare of the sun through the rinsed gray clouds would grow unbearable. You would have to move—to a different town, a milder clime—where the birds in the tree are not crows but morning doves or indigo buntings. But you do not throw the stone. You bury it deep inside you, folding color upon color until only darkness remains. Deeper than the crows can find.

Where Is It?

Now, you pause, hands pressing against the jambs, and lean into the entry. Your right foot hovers. Part of you has gone ahead, already inside, while another part hesitates. The stone door sill marking the entry glows, revealing its hidden story, a life underground. What does it want? To levitate? To loose its weight and become the white achene from an ancient cottonwood set free to drift in the summer air? Sometimes, when a boy, you walked in the woods behind your home until time broke into little pieces, too small to hear, and you wandered, almost weightless, trailing a possum or a badger toward something they wanted to show you, some story you almost remembered. When you returned, crossing from the woods back into the cultivated yard, it took a while to resume what had been your daily habits, to remember what you are.

The Story of Invention

This room approves your being here. The drawers in the bureau, full of their own memories and themselves seeking understanding, welcome you. In remote sites, men labor to extract precious minerals from the dark earth, then hide them again in underground labyrinths. So many mistakes, so many wrong turnings away from the morning light. The possibility of a nod from a distant father carrying you through all this wandering. And now, after years of clenching the stone, you let it slip free, and with it a long held breath. Stories return, of a father who, himself, struggled, and you tell them with pleasure. Your siblings nodding as they listen. The patience of crows brings you to this moment and the wooden floor sighs with pleasure beneath you.

Home is a Complete Sentence

Miriam Weinstein

Home.

The almost silent, breathy capital H.
Two solid pillars with a straight bar between them
like a rung on a ladder or a bridge.

Stability in two limbs.

And there you are: Half way up one side, resting.
Will you complete the precarious walk

across what now looks like a very thin balance beam?
Risk slipping and falling into the perfect circular pond

of the neighboring o? If you fall, will someone throw you
another smaller o, a life ring to float on, or a piece of the H
for support while you catch your breath?

Now, on the edge of the o, it's either back over to hang on
the ladder of H for safety, or time to move on.

Look at those two massive mountains of the m ahead of you,
three quarters of the way across the sentence. Home.
The trek along m is worth it.

You know what's on the other side. A swirl in the tail of e
where you can rest. Yet e is fraught with expectations

of embraces; or, at least half embraces
as the e stands there at the end—not fully closed.
But go on. Slide off

the e and then hop over that period.
Go on.

Begin your own sentence.

Neutralities

M.J. Iuppa

In obedience to a dream
the lake still moves at night.
Without dreaming, I move
in the corridor between home and water,
between wanting to cast aside tethers—
light as spider's silk, heavy as obedience.

It's hard to break ties in a dream.
To lift up dead weight and move
is a giant's wish …
I see myself dancing in the glassy surface—
two-stepping to monotonous laps—
the rasp: this way, this one way, home.

"Where in the World Did You Come from?"
Of Traveling, Oz, and Home

Mark Vinz

As many of us did, I grew up with adages, and the ones that made the strongest impression had to do with the place called *home.* As a child I learned that home is a man's castle (though I had to wonder where that left women and children); home, too, is where the heart is, where charity begins, where fires are to be kept burning (I also wondered about that one, for we had no fireplace; if our home could be on the range, where I desperately wanted it to be, there wouldn't be any problem keeping a roaring blaze going). The most familiar saying, of course, was "there's no place like home," which I've always associated with *The Wonderful Wizard of Oz*, my favorite childhood book, and a kind of touchstone I've carried into adulthood. Those words are actually quoted in the movie, not in the book (where Dorothy simply says "take me home to Aunt Em" as she clicks the heels of her magic shoes). But in *both* the book and the movie I had a very hard time understanding how Dorothy could give up the fairyland of Oz and her fabulous new friends there for the drab prairies—not to mention tornadoes—of Kansas. But that was long before I myself had lived in Kansas, before I had made enduring friendships or come to know what my own family truly meant to me.

There's no place like home, to be sure, though an important ambiguity resides here, especially for an adult. Sinclair Lewis' unrelenting satire of insularity and boosterism in *Main Street* comes to mind, as does Thomas Wolfe's frustrating dictum: *You Can't Go Home Again*. Depending on the interpreter, home can be a place of nurturing or a place of stunted growth, a repository of shaping, sustaining memory or a recurring nightmare. One thing seems certain: home for most of us is the place we spend all our lives re-imagining; if *it* doesn't change, *we* do, and vice versa. It's where we are and where we were, one endlessly played off against the other.

The place that I've called home for many years is the Red River Valley, the glacial bed of ancient Lake Agassiz on the Minnesota-North Dakota border. It's a very flat place, and in more than topography—homogeneously Scandinavian, Lutheran, conservative, reticent, and stand-offish, or so it appears to most outsiders. When I moved here in the late 60s, I indeed felt the Valley was populated with the kind of people I first read about in Dorothy's Kansas. Like Aunt Em and Uncle Henry, they "worked hard from morning till night and did not know what joy was." My view, of course, was destined to change immensely over time.

Still, I must admit that much of the time I've lived in the Valley I've tried in some way to maintain my own otherness—which, I suppose is my equivalent of saying I've been to Oz. I've somehow needed to see myself as an outsider, different from *them* in both attitude and demeanor. If their roots tend to be found in farms and small towns, mine are in cities; the Moorhead-Fargo community in which I reside is the largest place many of them have ever lived, but for me it's the smallest. I like to think I'm staying here by choice, while I know many of them will leave—the young, to the worlds of apparent opportunity in places such as the Twin Cities; the old, "snowbirds" fleeing the awful winters. The land itself helps support that feeling of separation. Prairie country can take a long time to accept you, to let you feel at home.

On the other hand, it *is* home—the place where I've helped to raise a family, the place I automatically say I'm from when asked. I do have roots here, too, even if it took me a while to embrace them. My parents grew up in small Minnesota and North Dakota towns and even lived in both Fargo and Moorhead briefly, in the 1930s. My ethnic heritage is likewise typical of this region: my mother was full-blooded Norwegian; my father was descended from Germans and Scots-Irish.

Also typical, unfortunately, is the way those roots have become obscured. My father's family shows few signs of its heritage, and while my mother's mother was fluent in Norwegian, my mother spoke only a few sentences of the language; her children know only a few words. Similarly, when I visit my childhood homes in Minneapolis or northeastern Kansas, it's increasingly difficult to believe I ever lived in those places, no matter how much nostalgia resides there or how much I seek to maintain connections.

Home, when it comes down to it, is largely a matter of perception, and a complicated mixture at that. It's not just where we are now vs. where we once were, but those important other places to which we've traveled in between. If learning a foreign language helps us understand our native tongues better, then what we bring back home after leaving is what can make the place come alive for us in ways we never imagined possible.

In my own experience, travels ranging from British Columbia to the British Isles have provided me with some radically different perceptions. Those "new eyes," so to speak, don't necessarily come from traveling.

Some years ago I taught a couple of summers in a local elderhostel, the theme of which was the native prairie. The elderhostelers, a lively and remarkable group, came from all over the U.S. Only a few had any connections to the Red River Valley, but all seemed very curious about something they tended to refer to as the "prairie mystique." How rare it is when *my* home is seen as exotic!

My part of the elderhostel teaching focused on how certain Midwestern authors have written about the prairies—from Ole Rolvaag and Willa Cather to contemporary writers such as Linda Hasselstrom and Paul Gruchow. Past or present, it's a literature of gains and losses, filled with extremes—from the pioneers' dizzying successes to the heartbreaking toll they paid, from the subtle beauty and promise of the landscape to the devastating harshness of the weather. We read about the prairie and, with guidance from my botanist co-teacher, we walked it, too—those few hundred acres of virgin land that remain around here—learning the names of wildflowers and other plants, letting imaginations run wild at centuries-old campsites and buffalo wallows. When we journeyed out under the immense prairie sky each day, I marveled at the changing attitudes, both theirs and mine. As never before, I recognized this place as home. I couldn't help but think of Dorothy from time to time. I thought, too, about the people who live here, and how the recent past has shown me again and again the ways they are not simply the undifferentiated, homogeneous mass I once thought they were. There *is* variety here—urban vs. rural, minority vs. majority, liberal vs. conservative—even though it may be, like the Midwestern landscape itself, a little slow to reveal itself. Indeed, homogeneity itself is a matter of perception, and when a place becomes too comfortable, as Dorothy learned, distinctions become blurred, as surely as they do for the casual passer-through bored by an apparent sameness.

Now, as I look back at these lines about *home* I've been rewriting and extending, I'm sitting in my room at Blue Cloud Abbey, a Benedictine monastery in northeastern South Dakota—a place where I often come to do some writing and which, for many other reasons, is a place that has become more important to me than just about any other. From these hills overlooking the Whetstone Valley, we can see a long way, more than thirty miles to the east, into Minnesota. Behind us, to the west, is a horizon of higher hills, a good place to consider perspectives in both space and time. It's truly amazing what a few hundred feet of elevation can do for the eyes, the same way that being a guest in a monastery can revive an inner world too easily overwhelmed in everyday work and busyness.

I read a lot at the monastery, too, which is something I tend to find easier to do away from home—away from the phone and TV set, from everything that *needs* to be done. One of the books I've been reading is a collection of short fiction by Maura Stanton, *The Country I Come From*, and what has stayed in my head is, ironically, a story called "Oz." It's set in my old hometown, Minneapolis, and deals with a young girl's first experience with tornado warnings. After the storm, which turns out not to be a full-fledged tornado, the young narrator surveys the wreckage caused by tree limbs blown through living and dining room windows and suddenly comes to realize the importance of her family to her. "This must be like the future," she says at the end of the story. "Your past did not blow away. It was you who blew away. You looked out the window and everything was different."

Perhaps that's it exactly—those times when we are given that necessary perspective we've lacked, when we somehow come to realize how stuck we can get in our day-to-day assumptions. It takes something else—a storm, a visitor, a change of scenery no matter how slight—to give us a small sense of whatever it is that's truly important, and which we too often fail to notice at all.

I return to that other story of Oz, L. Frank Baum's, and realize that each of the dozen or so times I've come back to it in my adulthood, it's given me something new. All those years ago when I encountered it as a child, I gained my first awareness of what *home* might possibly mean, and then, in later years, it somehow became connected to the power of *place* itself, as well as the power of words, and of imagination. More than any other book I can think of, it's given me a first—and continuing—sense of wanting to be a writer. Quite simply, it entranced me. I delighted in adding my own variations to the familiar story, and I couldn't get it out of my dreams. I went on to read—or read in—a couple of Baum's other Oz books, but they never had the same effects, perhaps because they were only about Oz, without the Kansas contrasts. They simply didn't appeal to my imagination in the same way. As Coleridge believed (quoted in a book being read aloud during dinner at the monastery), imagination has something to do with the "reconciliation of opposites." Baum, after all, was a prairie man (not just from his experience in Kansas, but in the Dakotas, too), and in spite of the enchanting fantasy world he created, he was probably the first writer I came across who dealt directly with familiar Midwestern landscapes—which is the territory that has preoccupied me in my own writing and editing for many years now.

So, if *The Wonderful Wizard of Oz* will always be about the drama of good versus evil and about how one learns to make a way in the world with the help of friends, it is also in some measure about perceptions—about growing and changing, about confronting who you are, which is based in some part *where you come from* in the largest sense of that phrase:

> Aunt Em had just come out of the house to water the cabbages when she looked up and saw Dorothy running toward her. "My darling child," she cried, folding the little girl in her arms and covering her face with kisses. "Where in the world did you come from?"
>
> "From the Land of Oz," said Dorothy gravely. "And here is Toto, too. And oh, Aunt Em! I'm so glad to be at home again!"

When I re-read those closing lines, I notice, perhaps for the first time, that Dorothy says "*at* home," and that's what takes me beyond the adage. Being *at* home is being at peace with the place and with yourself. That can only happen for Dorothy—and for me—when what once seemed so unutterably drab has come to life. It should mean more than simply "staying at home," too, more than simply acquiescing in our notions of that place, whatever it (or they) may be. After all, if Dorothy will always be at home in Kansas, she will always feel the urge to travel again too, won't she? In that sense, it means even if we're never fully able to resolve all those questions of home and homes, we can never take them for granted either. It means, finally, at home *or* away, struggling not to be blinded by what we fail to see.

Earlier version published in *North Dakota Quarterly*, Vol. 63, no 4, Fall 1996.

Works Cited

Baum, L. Frank. *The New Wizard of Oz*. Indianapolis: Bobbs-Merrill, 1944.

Stanton, Maura. *The Country I Come From*. Minneapolis: Milkweed Editions

House of Dreams and Stars and Life

Charlene Langfur

Today the house is like a lotus, singular, afloat, an artist's piece.

Later, deeper in the night, when I'm asleep, it's on the edge of unsettling land.
Part of it is a boat with float to it, a moveable vessel,
a safety net in the middle of what I try to imagine
is coming near. I hear the house in the night. Its voice. How it sounds in the dark
is different than in the day.
How it holds us in place in an expanding universe,
a touchstone, lone, readied, the spirit's guide.

This willowy fragile house that holds me in it,
house of dreams and stars and life, an ark of wishes,
a shelter to hold ideas in place and warm the body all at once,
decorated with lucky charms, iconic family pictures
a history of mysterious dreams
and lights in the window seen from far away.
How far? Gravity's angel. Earth. The dog hums. Tides magnetize.
Stories and shelters. A roof to keep it.
And this one, my own is dry, clear, plain.
An embrace of space. House.
A universe patched to another.
From the roof of the house in the night, I see each star, markers holding me in place
like Chinese lanterns in the summer, like charms in the pocket,
totems, tiny lights against an endless dark.

Earth's mantle, yes, Earth's shelter. It is always more.
Doors and windows. The planet's graces. We know
so much and even so still get lost, the love inside the house
disappeared, nearly gone while out for the afternoon.
In what room did it get lost? Turn sideways.
Clouds ascending. Water in the air. But the house is safe.
As I write this, it is. Worlds moving in orbit
and us aboard the vessel's back.

The simple of it keeps us balanced. Earth moves. The head tilts.
The tides rise. The dog's low deep sound, almost an alarm.
I listen, calm as a child, to the low orderly
music of the spheres. The house, not lost in space this day,
no flying off, no house with wings. It is not gone with a magician's snap
of his fingers. Thunder. Moon rise. Surprise bells on the porch in the night.
Stories on the land in the front yard, stories in the pocket.
House of earth dreams. Shelter in the night. Tonight the house is safe.

Notes on Contributors

Suzanne Allen is a Pushcart Prize nominee, published and anthologized in five countries and online at *Cider Press Review* and *Crack the Spine.* She co-edits *The Bastille: The Literary Magazine of Spoken Word Paris.* Her chapbook, *Verismilitude,* is available at CorruptPress.org.

John Azrak is the former English department chair at Walt Whitman high school on Long Island. He has published stories and poems in a wide variety of literary magazines and anthologies. New York is where his home and heart reside.

Cynthia M. Baer writes poetry from her cabin in the Santa Cruz mountains, a land whose geography has become home. Her unpublished collection of poems, *Fault Lines,* explores land and self, the ways in which the land—its geology and ecology—informs our being and directs us home.

Rachel Barenblat is the author of *70 Faces* (Phoenicia Publishing, 2011) and *Waiting to Unfold* (Phoenicia Publishing, 2013). She holds an MFA from Bennington College. Since 2003 she has blogged as The Velveteen Rabbi. She serves a small congregation in western Massachusetts where she lives with her husband and son.

Gary Boelhower's poems have appeared in many anthologies and journals. In 2012, he won the Foley Poetry Prize from *America* magazine. His most recent collection of poems, *Marrow, Muscle, Flight* won the Midwest Book Award. His website is www.gboelhower.com.

Jill Breckenridge has published three books of poetry: *How to Be Lucky* won the Bluestem Award, as judged by William Stafford; *Civil Blood* was nominated for the American Library Association's "Notable Books" of the year. Her third collection, *The Gravity of Flesh,* won a 2009 Northeastern Minnesota Book Award. Her memoir, *Miss Priss and the Con Man,* was published in 2011. She is now completing a collection entitled *The Sometimes Poems.*

Emily K. Bright holds an MFA in poetry from the University of Minnesota. Her chapbook, *Glances Back,* was published by Pudding House Press and her poems have appeared in *Other Voices International, North American Review,* and *The Pedestal Magazine.* Follow her commentaries on writing and social justice at http://emilykbright.blogspost.com.

Tami Mohamed Brown holds an MFA in creative writing from Hamline University and is the recipient of a 2011-12 Loft Mentor Series Award. Her writing appears regularly in the Minnesota Women's Press and has recently appeared in *Sweet, Literary Mama, Mizna,* and in the anthology *Open to Interpretation: Intimate Landscape.*

Wendy Brown-Báez has published prose and poetry in numerous literary journals as well as in the books *Ceremonies of the Spirit* and *Transparencies of Light.* The creator of "Writing Circles for Healing," she received McKnight and Minnesota State Arts Board grants to teach at risk youth and in non-profit organizations. Her website is www.wendybrownbaez.com.

Although he is best known for his Native American writing, **Joseph Bruchac**'s paternal ancestry is from Slovakia. Those Slovak roots have inspired many of his poems as well as his young adult novel *Dragon Castle* (Dial, 2012) and his Breakfast Serials novella *Janko and the Giant.*

Home for **Dan Campion** is Iowa City, where he moved from his hometown, Chicago, in 1978. He is the author of *Peter De Vries and Surrealism,* a coeditor of *Walt Whitman: The Measure of His Song,* and a contributor to *Light, Poetry, Shenandoah,* and many other publications.

Judith Waller Carroll's poetry has appeared in *Heron Tree, Naugatuck River Review, Umbrella, Stone's Throw Magazine* and has been nominated for the Best of the Net and won the 2010 Carducci Poetry Prize from the Tallahassee Writers Association. Her chapbook, *Walking in Early September,* is available from Finishing Line Press.

ROBIN CHAPMAN is the author of eight books of poetry, most recently *One Hundred White Pelicans* (Tebot Bach, 2013).

SHARON CHMIELARZ's latest book is *Love from the Yellowstone Trail* (North Star Press, 2013). Her website is www.sharonchmielarz.com.

JAN CHRONISTER teaches English and Creative Writing at Fond du Lac Tribal and Community College. She lives in the woods near Maple, Wisconsin. Her first chapbook, *Target Practice,* was published by Parallel Press at UW-Madison.

JAMES CIHLAR is the author of *Undoing* (Little Pear Press, 2008) and *Rancho Nostalgia* (Dream House Press, 2013).

DEBORAH COOPER is the author of five poetry collections, most recently *Under the Influence of Lilacs* (Clover Valley Press). She is the 2012-2014 Duluth Poet Laureate.

KAREN DONLEY-HAYES' work has appeared in numerous publications, including *Equus, Journal of the American Medical Association, Bartleby Snopes, Blue Lyra Review,* and *Chicken Soup for the Soul—My Cat's Life.* She lives in Ohio with her husband, several geriatric cats, a German shepherd, four hens, and one horse.

ALICE OWEN DUGGAN lives in Saint Paul, Minnesota with her husband where she cares for public and private gardens, and writes poems. Her first chapbook, *A Brittle Thing,* was published in 2012 by Greenfuse Press of Colorado.

CAROL DUNBAR lives with her family in an off-grid homestead in the woods of northern Wisconsin. She holds a BFA in theater arts and runs a small furniture business with her husband. She writes both fiction and nonfiction, including articles for print and online publication.

SUSAN ELBE is the author of *The Map of What Happened,* which won the 2012 Backwaters Press Prize, and *Eden in the Rearview Mirror* (Word Press), as well as two chapbooks: *Where Good Swimmers Drown,* winner of the Concrete Wolf Press 2011 chapbook Prize, and *Light Made from Nothing* (Parallel Press). Her website is www.susanelbe.com.

KAREN LYNN ERICKSON is a writer, composer, and professor of French at the College of St. Benedict/St. John's University, where she teaches courses in French language, literature, Biblical women, and the history of interpretation. She shares a love of music and creative expression with her children, Danny and Leah.

Born in Port-au-Prince, M. J. Fievre is an expat whose short stories and poems have appeared in numerous publications, including *Haiti Noir* (Akashic Books, 2011) and *The Beautiful Anthology* (TNB, 2012). She's the editor of *Sliver of Stone Magazine.*

Linda Nemec Foster is the author of nine poetry collections including *Amber Necklace from Gdansk* and *Talking Diamonds*. Her poems have also appeared in *Nimrod, Georgia Review, New American Writing,* and *North American Review*. She founded the Contemporary Writers Series at Aquinas College in Grand Rapids, Michigan.

Gloria Frym's recent books are *Mind Over Matter* and *Any Time Now*. She is also the author of two short story collections—*Distance No Object* and *How I Learned*—as well as many volumes of poetry, including *Homeless at Home*, which won an American Book Award. She teaches at California College of the Arts in the Bay area.

Vicki Graham has published two poetry collections: *The Tenderness of Bees* (2008), and *Alembic*, a finalist for the Minnesota Book Award, 2011. She was poet in residence at the H. J. Andrews Experimental Forest in 2006 and at Shotpouch Creek, 2012. Her poems have appeared in *Poetry, Midwest Quarterly, Seneca Review,* and other journals.

Keith Gunderson is Professor Emeritus in Philosophy, University of Minnesota. He is the author of a number of books in poetry and philosophy including *A Continual Interest in the Sun and Sea, Inland Missing the Sea,* and *Mentality and Machines.*

Jessica Erica Hahn was born in a renovated WWII tanker but grew up in San Francisco where she still lives. She studied creative writing at San Francisco State University and English Literature at UC Berkeley. Her website is www.jessicaericahahn.com.

Laura L. Hansen is a 1979 graduate of Concordia College and has been employed as an independent bookseller for the past 25 years. She lives in Little Falls, Minnesota and has self-published two poetry chapbooks, *Diving the Drop-off* and *Why I Keep Rabbits*. Her work has been published in regional journals and magazines.

Penny Harter is published widely in journals and anthologies. Her recent books include *One Bowl* (2012); *Recycling Starlight* (2010); *The Night Marsh* (2008). A featured reader at the 2010 Dodge Festival, she won three fellowships from the NJSCA, and Mary Carolyn Davies Award from the PSA, and a residency from VCAA (2010).

Margaret Hasse grew up in South Dakota, leaving to study English at Stanford University. The Twin Cities has been her home since 1973. Her fourth collection of poetry is *Earth's Appetite* (2013). Hasse is the recipient of a National Endowment for the Arts poetry fellowship and two Loft-McKnight grants.

Emily Ruth Hazel is a Dorothy Sargent Rosenberg Poetry Prize winner whose chapbook, *Body & Soul* (Finishing Line Press), was a New Women's Voices Finalist. Her poems have been commissioned by Spark and Echo Arts and have appeared in literary journals and anthologies. She studied Creative Writing at Oberlin College.

Roberta J. Hill, an Oneida poet, is the author of *Star Quilt, Philadelphia Flowers,* and *Cicadas: New & Selected Poems,* all from Holy Cow! Press. Her poetry is included in *Sing: Poetry from the Indigenous Americas* (2011) and *Bringing Gifts, Bringing News: Fifty Poems, Five Lines Each* (2011).

Born and raised in Connecticut, **Jill Hinners** now lives and writes in Duluth, Minnesota, where she dwells with her husband and nine-year-old son in their century-old house near the shores of Lake Superior. Her poetry has appeared in several regional anthologies.

Catherine Abbey Hodges is the author of *All the While,* a chapbook published by Finishing Line Press. Her poems have appeared in print and online venues including *The Southern Review, Verse Daily, Rock and Sling,* and *Canary.* She is a professor of English at Porterville College.

M.J. Iuppa lives on a small farm near the shores of Lake Ontario. She is writer-in-residence and Director of the Arts Minor Program at St. John Fisher College, Rochester, New York. Her recent prose chapbook, *Between Worlds,* was published by FootHills Publishing, 2013.

As editor of Many Voices Press, **Lowell Jaeger** compiled *New Poets of the American West,* an anthology of poets from 11 western states. He is the author of five poetry collections, including WE (Main Street Rag Press, 2010) and *How Quickly What's Passing Goes Past* (Grayson Books, 2013). Most recently, Jaeger was awarded the Montana Governor's Humanities Award for his work in promoting thoughtful civic discourse.

Framed by the window of her study, **Laura Jean** watches evening descend along the Minneapolis skyline filled with rooftops and an old elm tree, while swilling hot chocolate and writing.

Janet Jerve's first book of poetry, *Excavation,* was published by North Star Press in June, 2013. Her poems have appeared in *Poetry East, Water-Stone Review,* and *Emprise Review;* in anthologies *A Ghost at Heart's Edge,* published by North Atlantic Books and *Beloved on the Earth: 150 Poems of Grief and Gratitude,* published by Holy Cow! Press.

Linda Kantner is a social worker and infant mental health specialist working and writing in Saint Paul, Minnesota.

Molly Sutton Kiefer is the author of two chapbooks, *The Recent History of Middle Sand Lake* (winner of the 2010 Astonishing Beauty Ruffian Press Poetry Prize) and *City of Bears* (dancing girl press, 2013). Her website is www.mollysuttonkiefer.com.

From The Writing Project at Teacher's College to Manhattanville College to her own living room, **Drew Lamm** leads writers onto the page to discover and hone their unique voices. She helps clients honour their stories and find and relish the meaning, joy and poetic in their lives. She is also a published author.

Julie Landsman is a retired teacher, memoir and fiction writer and editor. She has great faith in poetry and its power to create a home in her classrooms. She continues to work with children and teachers in many public schools, to bring their stories into the world.

Keiko Lane is a poet, essayist, and psychotherapist. In addition to her literary writing, which has been published in journals and anthologies, she also writes essays about intersections of queer culture, oppression resistance and liberation psychology. She lives in Berkeley, CA where she maintains a private psychotherapy practice and teaches graduate psychology and cultural studies.

Charlene Langfur is an organic gardener, a southern Californian, and a Syracuse University graduate writing Fellow. Her most recent publications include work in *The Stone Canoe, The Toronto Quarterly, Assisi, Steam Ticket, Ninepaton,* and *The Hampden-Sydney Poetry Review.* She has two eBooks online.

Katie Hae Leo is a writer and performer whose work has appeared in *Water-Stone Review, Kartika Review, Asian American Literary Review,* and *Asian American Poetry and Writing.* Her chapbook, *Attempts at Location,* was a finalist for the Tupelo Snowbound Award and is available through Finishing Line Press.

J. Patrick Lewis' first book of adult poetry, *Gulls Hold Up the Sky,* was publishing by Laughing Fire Press, 2010. His poems have appeared in *Gettysburg Review, New England Review,* and many others. He has published over 80 children's picture/poetry books with Knopf, Little, Brown, National Geographic, Chronicle, and others. He is the Poetry Foundation's U.S. Children's Poet Laureate, 2011-2013.

Joyce Lombard lives in Venture, California where she is a psychotherapist, artist, and poet, who particularly likes having a voice in anthologies. She has been published in Papier-Mache anthologies and Her Mark. She also teaches workshops based in the creative process, the most recent one on Memoir in 3D.

Professor of English and Director of Creative Writing at Lock Haven University, **Marjorie Maddox** has published eight poetry collections, two children's books, and over 450 stories, essays, and poems in journals and anthologies. She is the recipient of numerous awards and co-edited *Common Wealth: Contemporary Poets on Pennsylvania.* Please visit www.lhup.edu/mmaddoxh/biography.htm

The poetry of **John Manesis**, a retired physician, has appeared in over 75 literary publications, including *Wisconsin Review, Zone 3, North Dakota Quarterly, California State Poetry Quarterly,* and *Colere.* His fourth and most recent book is *In the Third Season,* published in 2012.

Freya Manfred has published seven collections of poetry including *My Only Home; Swimming with a Hundred Year Old Snapping Turtle,* which won the 2009 Booksellers' Choice Award; and *The Blue Dress.* She is the recipient of a Radcliffe/Harvard grant in poetry.

Farzana Marie grew up in Chile, California and Kazukhstan, to later spend years in Afghanistan as a civilian volunteer and Air Force officer. She writes poems and serves as President of the nonprofit Civil Vision International while studying for a Ph.D. in Persian Literature at the University of Arizona.

Fran Markover lives in Ithaca, New York where she works as a family therapist/addictions counselor. Recent honors include a Pushcart Prize nomination and a Constance Sattonstall residency. Her poems have been included in the journals *Calyx, Rattle, Runes, Karamu,* and *Cider Press Review.*

Ann McGovern is a prize-winning author of over 55 books for children. Her classic *Stone Soup* has been in print since 1967. Her books have sold over 25 million copies. Ann's poetry chapbook, *Drawing Outside the Lines,* was released in 2009. *River of Glass,* her full length collection, was published in 2011.

Heather McGrew has been a writing instructor at the University of Wisconsin-Superior for twelve years. In addition, she was the 1999 recipient of the Tom Kuster Creative Writing Award for Poetry. Her recent work has appeared in *Emerge Literary Journal, Red River Review, Turtle Way* and the *Penwood Review.*

Ethna McKiernan is the author of three poetry collections, most recently, *Sky Thick With Fireflies* (Salmon Poetry, Ireland, 2012). She is widely anthologized in collections as diverse as *The Notre Dame Anthology of Irish American Poetry, 33 Minnesota Poets,* and *Beloved on the Earth: 150 Poems of Grief and Gratitude.* She has twice been awarded a Minnesota State Arts Board Fellowship.

Elisabeth Murawski is the author of *Zorba's Daughter,* which won the 2010 May Swenson Poetry Award, *Moon and Mercury,* and two chapbooks. She was a Hawthornden Fellow in 2008.

Amy Nash received a B.A. in English Literature and studied with Annie Dillard at Wesleyan University. She also completed the Loft Literary Center's Foreword apprenticeship program. Her poems have appeared in numerous publications, including *Common Ground Review,* and she has given readings at several venues and on Minnesota Public Radio.

Naomi Shihab Nye lives with her husband, photographer Michael Nye, in a 110-year-old vernacular Victorian cottage with a big front porch and swing, in the heart of old downtown San Antonio.

Sheila Packa has published three books of poems: *The Mother Tongue, Echo & Lightning,* and *Cloud Birds.* Her website is www.sheilapacka.com.

Julia Morris Paul's poems have been published in various journals both national and international. She was a 2011 finalist for the May Swenson and the Blue Lynx Poetry Prizes. She serves on the boards of the Connecticut Poetry Society and Riverwood Poetry Series and is an elder law attorney in Manchester, Connecticut.

Penny Perry grew up on a family farm in Spooner, Wisconsin and has lived in Duluth, Minnesota for over thirty-five years. Her mother retired from doing alterations many years ago but, at 87, she stills sews every day for fun.

David Pichaske, Professor of English at Southwest Minnesota State University, has received Fulbright teaching fellowships to Poland, Latvia, and Mongolia. His books include *Song of the North Country: A Midwest Framework to the Songs of Bob Dylan* (Continuum, 2010) and *Ghosts of Abandoned Capacity* (Lambert Academic Publishing, 2012). His website is www.davidpichaske.com.

Marge Piercy's eighteenth poetry collection, *The Hunger Moon: New & Selected Poems,* was published in a paperback edition by Alfred Knopf in 2012. Her recent novel is *Sex Wars.* PM Press has republished *Dance the Eagle to Sleep* and *Vida,* with new introductions. Her memoir is *Sleeping with Cats* (Harper Perennial).

Nadine Pinede is the daughter of Haitian immigrants. She holds degrees from Harvard, Oxford (where she was a Rhodes Scholar) and Indiana University. She is the author of a poetry chapbook, *An Invisible Geography* (Finishing Line Press, 2012). Her fiction appears in *Haiti Noir* (Akashic Books, 2011) and her memoir in *Becoming: Anthology of Women's Stories* (University of Nebraska Press, 2012).

Kenneth Pobo had a chapbook, *Save My Place,* published by Finishing Line Press in 2012. He has work forthcoming in *Two Thirds North, Revolver, Crannog,* and *The Same.*

Andrea Potos is the author of four poetry collections, including *We Lit the Lamps Ourselves* (Salmon Poetry), and *Yaya's Cloth* (Iris Press). Her poems appear widely online and in print.

Bruce Pratt's novel *The Serpents of Blissfull,* was published by Mountain State Press in 2011. His poetry collection *Boreal,* is available from Antrim House Books; his short fiction, poetry, and drama have appeared in dozens of journals in the United States, Canada, Europe, and won numerous awards.

Judith Prest is a poet, artist, teacher and creativity coach. Her work has been published in several anthologies and literary journals. She has also published two full length collections of her work—*Late Day Light* and *Sailing on Spirit Wind,* both from Spirit Wind Books. She lives in Duanesburg, New York.

Claudia M. Reder teaches at California State University at Channel Islands. Her chapbook, *Uncertain Earth* (Finishing Line Press), is available on Kindle.

George Roberts lives and writes in North Minneapolis. With his wife and partner Beverly, he runs Homewood Studios, an art gallery, home for local artists and community gathering place.

Kristina Roth recently returned to live in California with her family, after a long time in Houston. She still considers South Dakota to be her home. Her essays have appeared in a number of literary journals.

As surprised as **Sherry Rovig** is to be in her sixth decade, the phenomenon of accelerated time is losing its cachet. She practices being present and is sometimes compelled to write, as well as witness.

Blue Light Press published **Mary Kay Rummel**'s sixth poetry book, *What's Left is the Singing.* Other books include *Love in the End* and *The Illuminations.* A recent award is the Irish American Crossroads Prize. Retired from the University of Minnesota, Duluth, she teaches part time at California State University, Channel Islands, commuting between the two states.

Kenneth Salzmann's poems have appeared in such journals as *Rattle, Sow's Ear Poetry Review, Comstock Review* and anthologies including *Reeds and Rushes: Pitch, Buzz, and Hum; Beloved on the Earth: 150 Poems of Grief and Gratitude,* and *Riverine: An Anthology of Hudson Valley Writers.* His website is www.kensalzmann.com.

Ellie Schoenfeld is a poet native to Duluth, Minnesota. She is the author of three poetry collections, *Screaming Red Gladiolus!* (Poetry Harbor, 1999), *Difficult Valentines* (Fallow Deer Books, 2004), and *The Dark Honey: New & Used Poems* (Clover Valley Press, 2009). Her work has been published in an anthology, *The Moon Rolls Out of Our Mouths* (Calyx Press, 2005).

Ellen Shriner is published in the anthology *Mourning Sickness* and in *Wisconsin Review, BrainChild, Midwest Home* and other journals. She writes for *WordSisters* (wordsisters.wordpress.com) and hopes to publish *Colette's Legacy,* a coming-of-age-in-the-workplace memoir set in the 1970s. She lives in Saint Paul, Minnesota with her husband and two grown children.

Joseph A. Soldati lives in Portland, Oregon and has published numerous poems and essays in a variety of literary journals, magazines, and anthologies, including *New Millennium Writings, America Magazine* and the anthology *Beloved on the Earth: 150 Poems of Grief and Gratitude.* His latest chapbook, *On Account of Darkness,* was published in 2011.

John Sorensen was born in Saint Paul, Minnesota. A lifetime of editorial and writing work, principally at Augsburg Publishing House in Minneapolis, was followed by a move to Duluth's Central Hillside, where John and his wife Cyndy happily watch lightning storms over Wisconsin and the ships arriving at the Duluth-Superior harbor.

Amy Jo Swing has been writing poetry seriously since ninth grade algebra. Since then, she has been blessed to receive a McKnight/Loft poetry grant as well as several poetry contest awards and writing retreat stays. She lives and works in Duluth, Minnesota with her partner and their two daughters.

Thom Tammaro lives and works in Moorhead, Minnesota. He is the author of two collections of poems, *Holding on for Dear Life* and *When the Italians Came to My Home Town,* and two chapbooks, *Minnesota Suite* and *31 Mornings in December.* He is the recipient of three Minnesota Book Awards for anthologies he has edited.

Gregory Tuleja is the Academic Dean at the Williston Northampton School in Eastampton, Massachusetts, where he also teaches ninth grade English and coaches the girls cross country team. He has published many poems and short stories in various journals and magazines.

Mark Vinz is Professor Emeritus of English at Minnesota State University, Moorhead. His work has appeared in numerous magazines and anthologies; his most recent books are poetry collections, *The Work is All,* and *In Harm's Way.* He is also the co-editor of several anthologies, including *Inheriting the Land: Contemporary Voices from the Midwest.*

Connie Wanek is the author of three collections of poetry, and is a Witter Bynner Fellow of the Library of Congress. She lives in Duluth, Minnesota, but remembers "home" in New Mexico, too.

Cary Waterman is a poet and creative nonfiction writer. Her most recent book, *Book of Fire,* was a finalist for the Midwest Book Award. She teaches in the Augsburg College MFA Program.

Karen Herseth Wee is a longtime Minnesota writer and co-founder in the early 1970s of *Northfield Women Poets*, still active today and renamed *Penchant*. She co-edited three of *Penchant*'s four anthologies—in 1984, 1986, 1995, and 2007. Her *Book of Hearts* was a 1994 finalist for the Minnesota Book Award. She is grounded by a South Dakota prairie perspective; her birth home is the ranch house described in her poem "The Heart of the Matter."

Kathleen Weihe is the author of *Unless You Count Birds,* a collection of poetry. She teaches composition at Anoka-Ramsey Community College, and has taught poetry at The Loft Literary Center. She received an artist's assistance fellowship from the Minnesota State Arts Board and a Loft-McKnight Award for poetry. She lives in Minneapolis.

Elizabeth Weir grew up in England and lives in Minnesota. She received three SASE awards and a SASE-Jerome award. Her work appears in the anthology *Beloved on the Earth: 150 Poems of Grief and Gratitude, Water-Stone Review, Turtle Lit, American Poetry Quarterly* and *White Pelican Review.*

Miriam Weinstein is enrolled in the Loft Literary Center's apprenticeship program in poetry, *Foreword.* She has M.Ed. degrees in Adult Education, Family Life Education, and a B.A. in Dramatic Arts. Miriam has worked as an actress, photographer, educational program planner, and parent educator. She lives in Minneapolis.

Sarah Brown Weitzman has had three hundred poems published in numerous journals and anthologies. She received an award for "Excellence in Poetry" from the National Endowment for the Arts. Her latest book, *Herman and the Ice Witch*, is available from Main Street Rag.

J. P. White has published five books of poetry, two with Holy Cow! Press, and one novel, *Every Boat Turns South.*

Martin Willitts Jr., retired Senior Librarian, lives in Syracuse, New York. His most recent full length collection is *The Heart Knows, Simply, What it Needs* (Aldrich Press, 2012). He has six forthcoming collections, including his National Wild Earth Poetry Contest winning collection *Searching for What is Not There* (Hiraeth Press, 2013).

Morgan Grayce Willow's collections and chapbooks include *Between, Silk, The Maps are Words,* and *Arpeggio of Appetite.* Her awards include grants from the Minnesota State Arts Board, McKnight Foundation, and Witter Bynner Foundation. "Corn Rows" is from her collection *Dodge & Scramble,* forthcoming from Ice Cube Press in October, 2013.

Rosemary Winslow is a professor at The Catholic University of America in Washington, D.C. where she lives with her husband artist John Winslow. She is the recipient of three Larry Neal Awards, several grants and has published numerous poems, essays, and book chapters on poetry and teaching writing.

Jane Yolen has published more than 325 books, including five books of adult poetry, two of which are from Holy Cow! Press: *Things to Say to a Dead Man* and *Ekaterinoslav: One Family's Passage to America, a Memoir in Verse.*

Permissions and Sources

We wish to express our thanks to authors, editors and publishers and other copyright holders for their permission to include the works indicated below.

"Postcard to Ailene from a Place in the Air," by Suzanne Allen, first appeared in *San Pedro River Review,* Spring, 2012, reprinted by permission of the author.

"The Hot Corner," by John Azrak, first appeared in *Coe Review,* reprinted by permission of the author.

"The Permeable World," by Rachel Barenblat, appeared in an earlier version at the blog *Velveteen Rabbi,* reprinted by permission of the author.

"Nesting," by Gary Boelhower, first appeared in *Marrow, Muscle, Flight* by Gary Boelhower, published by Wildwood River Press, 2011, and reprinted by permission of the author.

"Drawing of My Family: Age Six," by Jill Breckenridge, is from *How to Be Lucky* by Jill Breckenridge (winner of the 1990 Bluestem Award) and reprinted by permission of the author.

"A Hundred Things," by Emily K. Bright, was first published in the *North American Review* (April, 2006) and reprinted by permission of the author.

"Lands of Song," by Joseph Bruchac, was previously published in *The Connecticut Review,* and reprinted by permission of the author.

"Back in Your Old House in Montana," by Judith Waller Carroll, was previously published in the chapbook *Walking in Early September* (Finishing Line Press, 2012) and reprinted by permission of the author.

"Hometown," by Robin Chapman, originally appeared in *the eel grass meadow* (Tebot Bach, 2011). Copyright © 2011 by Robin Chapman and reprinted with her permission.

"Fixing Potato Salad While the Past Comes and Goes," by Sharon Chmielarz, is reprinted by permission of the author and North Star Press.

"The House Made of Words," by James Cihlar, is reprinted from *Undoing* by James Cihlar (Little Pear Press, 2008) by permission of the author.

"The Avid Heirs of the Farm," by Alice Owen Duggan, was published in the Fall, 2006, Volume 9 issue of *Water-Stone Review,* and reprinted by permission of the author.

"Five Summer Nights," by Susan Elbe, first appeared in *MARGIE Review* (Fall 2008, Vol. 7) and in *The Map of What Happened* (Blackwaters Press, 2013), winner of the 2012 Blackwaters Prize, and reprinted by permission of the author.

"The Home Stretch," by Karen Lynn Erickson, appeared in the *Lower Stumpf Lake Review,* and is reprinted by permission of the author.

"Foreshocks," by M. J. Fievre, previously appeared on *The Nervous Breakdown* and is reprinted by permission of the author.

"Home," by Gloria Frym, originally appeared in *Encyclopedia Project, Vol. II, F-K* (Encyclomedia, 2010) and reprinted by permission of the author.

"Blacklock," by Vicki Graham, is reprinted from *The Storm Petrel, Vol. 34, Number 3, 2011,* by permission of the author.

"The Stradivaris in the Locker," by Keith Gunderson, is reprinted from *3142 Lyndale Avenue South, Apt. 34* (Minnesota Writers Publishing House, 1975) by permission of the author.

"Passing Through? Squatting is Another Name for Home," by Jessica Erica Hahn, was first published in a different, longer version as "Passing Through? One Woman's Experience Squatting in America" in *Prime Mincer,* #1.3, Winter, 2011 and reprinted by permission of the author.

"What Holds Me," by Laura L. Hansen, is reprinted from *The Talking Stick, Volume 18* (Common Threads, 2009) by permission of the author.

"Shelling Peas," by Penny Harter, first appeared on *Jama Rattigan's Alphabet Soup* blog at: jamarattigan.com/2101/06/03friday-feast-two-poetic-peas-in-a-pod. It is reprinted by permission of the author.

"Prairie World and Wanderer," by Margaret Hasse, was published previously in the *South Dakota Review* and included in *Earth's Appetite* by Margaret Hasse (Nodin Press). It is reprinted by permission of the author.

"Safe," by Catherine Abbey Hodges, first appeared in *All the While* by Catherine Abbey Hodges (Finishing Line Press) and is reprinted by permission of the author.

"Neutralities," by M. J. Iuppa, was first published in *Yankee* and then collected in *Night Traveler* (FootHills Publishing, 2003) and reprinted by permission of the author.

"Now It's a House," by Lowell Jaeger, was previously published in *Suddenly Out of a Long Sleep* (Arctos Press, 2009) and copyrighted by Lowell Jaeger. It is reprinted by permission of the author.

"Coming Home," by Janet Jerve, was first published in *Excavation* (North Star Press, 2013) and is reprinted by permission of the author.

"A Shelter Is not a Home," by Linda Kantner, was previously included in *Sacred Ground: Writings about Home* (Milkweed Editions, 1996), and is reprinted by permission of the author.

"Settled," by Marjorie Maddox, was previously published in Missing Spokes Press anthology (1999); *American Jones Building & Maintenance*, and is reprinted by permission of the author.

"Displaced Person," by John Manesis, is included in *In the Third Season* (2012) and is reprinted by permission of the author.

"The Horror of the World Around," by Freya Manfred, first appeared in *My Only Home* (Red Dragonfly Press) and is reprinted by permission of the author.

"75 ½ Bedford Street, The Edna St. Vincent Millay House," by Ann McGovern, was previously published in *Carquinez Poetry Review* and is reprinted by permission of the author.

"Relearning Home," by Heather McGrew, appeared orginally in a slightly different version in Ms. McGrew's Master of Arts thesis *Lessons in Cartography: A Collection of Essays* (2000). It is reprinted by permission of the author.

"Dear God of H__________," by Ethna McKiernan, appears in *Sky Thick With Fireflies* (Salmon Poetry, Ireland, 2012) and is reprinted by permission of the author.

"Child with Reader," by Elisabeth Murawski, first appeared in *ellipsis . . . literature & art* (2012) and is reprinted by permission of the author.

"Any evening in early December, " by Marge Piercy, first appeared in *Paterson Literary Review,* Volume 40, 2012 and is reprinted by permission of the author.

"Provenance," by Nadine Pinede, first appeared in *An Invisible Geography* by Nadine Pinede (Finishing Line Press, 2012) and is reprinted by permission of the author.

"A Gay Doll House," by Kenneth Pobo, appears in the *Evening Street Review* (2012) and *Peeks and Valleys,* Volume 8, 2008, and is reprinted by permission of the author.

"Origins," by Andrea Potos, appears in *Yaya's Cloth* by Andrea Potos (Iris Press, 2007) and is reprinted by permission of the author.

"A Distant Ship Tiding Home," by Bruce Pratt, appears in e*llipsis . . . a journal of literature & art,* where it won the 2007 poetry prize and is also included in *Boreal* by Bruce Pratt (Antrim House Books, 2007) and is reprinted by permission of the author.

"Land," by Judith Prest, was first published in *Late Day Light* by Judith Prest (Spirit Wind Books, P.O. Box 15, Duanesbury, NY 12056) in 2011, and reprinted by permission of the author.

"The Meaning of Things," by Claudia M. Reder, was published in *Arsenic Lobster* and reprinted by permission of the author.

"Directions Home," by Kristina Roth, previously appeared in *Blueline* (Volume XXXI, 2010, SUNY-Potsdam) and is reprinted by permission of the author.

"The Persistence of Ashes," by Kenneth Salzmann, first appeared in *Front Range Review* (Spring, 2007) and is reprinted by permission of the author.

"Toward Moorhead, Minnesota," by Thom Tammaro, is reprinted from *Holding on for Dear Life* (Spoon River Poetry Press, 2004). Copyright 2004 By Thom Tammaro and reprinted by his permission.

"'Where in the World Did You Come from'? Of Traveling, Oz, and Home," by Mark Vinz, first appeared as an earlier version published in *North Dakota Quarterly,* Volume 63, Number 4, Fall, 1996, and reprinted by permission of the author.

"Pecans," by Connie Wanek, first appeared in *Water-Stone Review* and then included in *On Speaking Terms* by Connie Wanek (Copper Canyon Press, 2010), and reprinted by permission of the author.

"Horizon," by Cary Waterman, was previously published in *Rkvry Quarterly Literary Journal* (January, 2013) and is reprinted by permission of the author.

"The Heart of the Matter," by Karen Herseth Wee, was published in *The Book of Hearts* (Black Hat Press, 2003) and is reprinted by permission of the author.

"Looking Back," by Sarah Brown Weitzman, was first published in *Rattle,* Number 11, 1999, and is reprinted by permission of the author.

"Mending the Net," by Martin Willitts, Jr., first appeared in *Traveling Poets Society* and is reprinted by permission of the author.

"Going Home," by Rosemary Winslow, was first published in *The Southern Review* and reprinted in *The Breath of Parted Lips: Voices from the Robert Frost Place,* Volume 2. It is reprinted by permission of the author.

About the Editors

Jim Perlman's first home was in Minneapolis where his interest in poetry began in high school. In 1977, after editing various local literary magazines, he founded Holy Cow! Press. He edited the poetry anthology *Brother Songs: A Male Anthology of Poetry* (1979) and, with Ed Folsom and Dan Campion, co-edited *Walt Whitman: The Measure of His Song* (1981, rev. ed., 1997). He and his family moved to Duluth, Minnesota in 1988, where he co-founded the Spirit Lake Poetry series, and helped establish the Duluth poet laureate project in 2005. With co-editors Deborah Cooper, Mara Hart, and Pamela Mittlefehldt, *Beloved on the Earth: 150 Poems of Grief & Gratitude* was published in 2009.

Deborah Cooper has been writing poetry for over twenty years and has worked collaboratively with visual artists, musicians and dancers. She and her husband, Joel, who is a printmaker, have exhibited their collaborative images throughout the Midwest. Deborah co-edited the anthology *Beloved on the Earth: 150 Poems of Grief & Gratitude* (Holy Cow! Press) and she frequently teaches writing classes for those who are grieving the loss of a loved one. She also teaches Sacred Poetry classes, and mentors inmates at the St Louis County Jail. Deborah is the author of five collections of poems, most recently *Under the Influence of Lilacs* published by Clover Valley Press. She is the 2012-2014 Duluth Poet Laureate.

Mara Hart has been a university librarian, has taught English and Women's Studies at the University of Minnesota, Duluth, and has been a poetry editor of three literary periodicals. She writes memoirs in poetry and prose, teaches memoir writing, edits, and mentors writers. She edited *Lovecraft's New York Circle* published by Hippocampus Press, New York, in 2007, and was a co-editor of *Beloved on the Earth*, published by Holy Cow! Press. Her most recent book, *So Many Lovely Days*, was published by Kirk Press in 2013.

Pamela Mittlefehldt is a poet, writer, editor, and fiddler who has found home in Duluth, Minnesota. She is Professor Emerita of American Studies/Community Studies at St. Cloud State University, where she taught courses on place, diversity, sustainable communities, and creativity. She is revising a mystery, working on a collection of essays about the meaning of place, and beginning a cross-genre project on the body as place. The focus of her work is on the power of story to transform our lives as individuals and as communities.

About the Cover Artist

Throughout a career that took him from Chippewa City, Minnesota to New York and Paris, **George Morrison** (1919-2000) developed an aesthetic that proved to be an essential part in Modernism and Abstract Expressionism. It was during this time that Morrison made a place for himself within the canon of this critical period in American art, befriending other prominent artists such as Jackson Pollock and Willem de Kooning along the way. After returning to the United States, Morrison continued to create and exhibit his work on the East Coast, a period of time which also included a prominent teaching position at the Rhode Island School of Design. He made his way back to Minnesota, where he taught at the University of Minnesota and eventually returned to the North Shore area to retire from teaching and to focus on artmaking. Despite the faraway places to which his work took him, his imagery and sculptures commonly take as a point of reference the horizon line of the Midwestern landscape, particularly Lake Superior.